Quilt Toppings

Fun and Fancy Embellishment Techniques

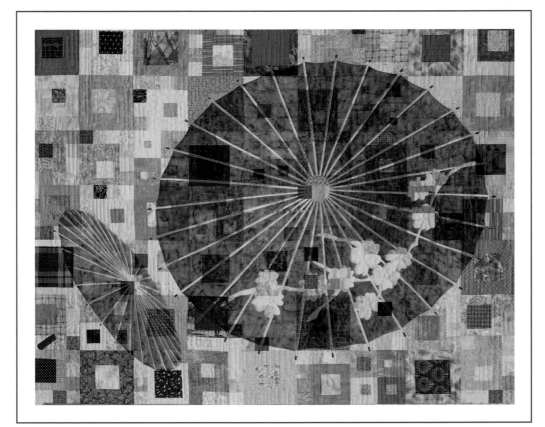

MELODY CRUST

Breckling Press

LIBRARY OF CONGRESS CATALOGING IN PUBLICATION DATA

Crust, Melody.

    Quilt toppings : fun and fancy embellishment techniques /
Melody Crust.

        p. cm.

    Includes index.

    ISBN 1-933308-02-8

    1. Fancy work. 2. Quilting. I. Title.

    TT750.C95 2005

    746.46—dc22

                          2005016829

This book was set in Neutraface and Sabon by Bartko Design, Inc.
Editorial and production direction by Anne Knudsen
Art direction, cover, and interior design by Kim Bartko
Photography by Charles Crust
Technical drawings by Kathryn Wagar Wright

Published by Breckling Press
283 Michigan Ave., Elmhurst,
IL 60126 USA

Printed and bound in China.

International Standard Book Number: 1-933308-02-8

DEDICATION

To the two people in my life who I most love—

to my husband Charles Crust for his

never-failing support and patient photography;

and to my sister Heather Osterman, who

always applauds and encourages me

in everything I do.

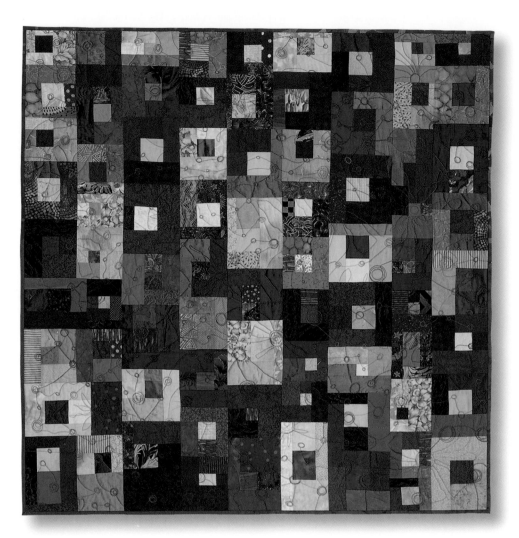

Fear No Color*. See page 101.*

Acknowledgments

My special thanks to Carol Castaldi,

Pat Michelsen, Christine Palmer, J.B. Scarf,

Kay Taylor, and Heather Waldron for generously

lending their amazing and beautiful quilts

to include in Quilt Toppings.

CONTENTS

PREFACE   1

1 PAINTS, CRAYONS, INKS, FOIL, AND MORE

PAINT, GLORIOUS PAINT   6

Prep Work and Supplies   6
Acrylic Craft Paints   8
Fabric Paints   9
Spray Paints   11
Painting Yardage   11
Stamping with Paints   13

PAINT STICKS   14

Prep Work and Supplies   15
Working with Paint Sticks   15

CRAYONS   16

Prep Work   16
Crayon Rubbings   18

MARKING PENS   18

Prep Work and Supplies   19
Lettering with Markers   19
Freehand Designs   20

ALL-PURPOSE INKS   20

Prep Work and Supplies   21

FOILING   22

Prep Work and Supplies   22
Getting Ready for Foil   22
Foil Adhesives   23
Applying Foil with Heat   24

STENCILING   25

IDEA GALLERY   28

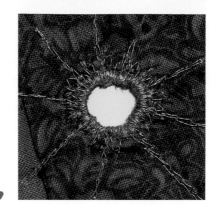

2 BEADS, BUTTONS, and MORE

BEADS 38

Prep Work and Supplies 38
Bead Placement 42
Beading by Hand 43
Beading by Machine 47

BEYOND BEADS: PEARLS, SEQUINS, JEWELS, AND SHI-SHAS 50

Prep Work and Supplies 50
Pearls 50
Sequins 51
Sew-On Jewels 53
Shi-sha Mirrors 54

HOT-FIX CRYSTALS 55

BUTTONS 56

Prep Work and Supplies 56
Selecting Buttons 57
Creative Button Embellishments 57
Decorating Button Holes 59

IDEA GALLERY 60

3 RIBBON, RICK RACK, AND MORE

RIBBON 70

Prep Work and Supplies 71
Ribbon Types 72
Ribbon Applications 76
Sewing with Ribbon 81

RICK RACK, BIAS TAPE, TRIM, CORDS, AND TASSELS 81

Prep Work and Supplies 81
Rick Rack 82
Bias Tape 82
Fringe 83
Cords 83
Tassels 84
Caring for Trim-Embellished
   Projects 85

EMBELLISHING WITH FABRIC 85

Prep Work and Supplies 85
Doilies 86
Handkerchiefs 86
Lace 87
Velvet 87
Lamé Fabrics 88
Silk 88
Polyester 88
Ultra-Suede 89

THREE-DIMENSIONAL EFFECTS 90

Prairie Points 90
Fabric Ruching 90
Gathered Fabric 90
Yo-Yos 91

IDEA GALLERY 92

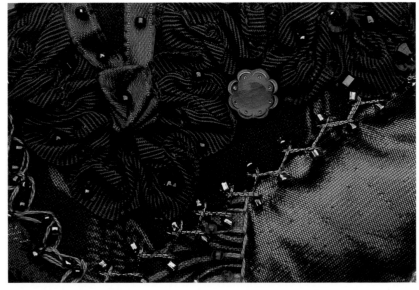

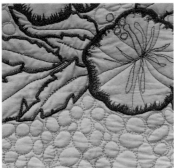

4 THREAD PLAY!

MACHINE STITCHING   98

Prep Work and Supplies   98
Selecting Machine Threads   99
Selecting Machine Needles   103
Stabilizing Your Fabric   108

MACHINE STITCHING TECHNIQUES   110

Machine Applique   110
Machine Embroidery   110
Redesign Your Fabric—with Thread   111
Machine Sashiko   112
Machine Couching   112
Crazy Quilting by Machine   113
Stitching from the Bobbin   114
Caring for Machine-Stitched Projects   115

HAND STITCHING   115

Prep Work and Supplies   116
Selecting Hand-Sewing Threads   116
Selecting Hand-Sewing Needles   117

HAND SEWING TECHNIQUES   119

Hand Appliqué   119
Hand Embroidery   121
Hand Sashiko   123
Hand Couching   123
Crazy Quilting by Hand   123
Caring for Hand-Stitched Projects   123

IDEA GALLERY   124

RESOURCES   131

INDEX   133

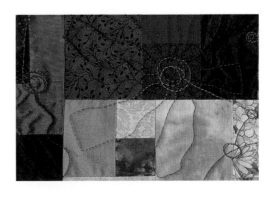

Imperial Flowers. *See page 15.*

PREFACE

Making a quilt is like baking a cake—sometimes all of the fun is in the frosting! You can have an incredibly good time embellishing your quilt in a thousand ways, many of which are sure to be new to you. If you've never thought to try paint, ink, or other color on your fabrics or even on the surface of an otherwise "finished" quilt top, then *Quilt Toppings* has surprises aplenty in store. In kindergarten you took enthusiastic delight in expressing your creativity with paint. Well, all those good times are waiting for you to come back to them! We will talk about what you need to know about painting tools and materials, share all the tricks and shortcuts, show you lots and lots of examples, and invite you to dive right in.

Beads, buttons, sequins, rhinestones, jewels, and shi-shas. Now that's a tempting list of goodies. There is an amazing variety of easy ways to incorporate these little beauties into your work. All you need are a threaded needle and a willing hand. Quilts are like people; some like to just let their natural loveliness shine through, while others long to be dressed to the nines and won't settle for less!

We will take a fresh look at some perennial favorites for embellishment— ribbons, lace, trims, tassels, and a host of fancy fabrics. Make your own cords in any color or material you please . . . learn brand new ways to use beautiful old

Painted fabric. See page 8.

All Dressed for School. *See page 66.*

Fairyland. See page 98.

Pears. See page 14.

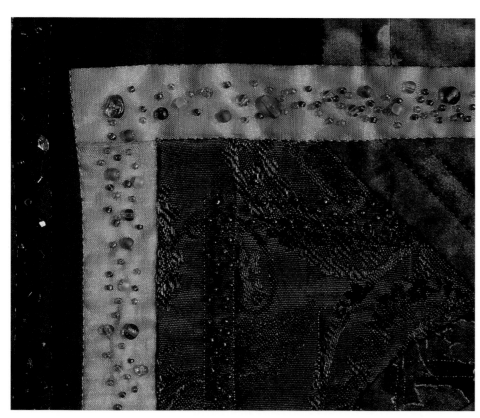

1936. See page 44.

English Tea. See page 122.

Beauties in a Basket. *See page 91.*

hankies . . . emboss velvet . . . decorate your quilt with flowers . . . have fun with yo-yos (the fabric kind) . . . the list goes on and on. You will be absolutely amazed at how fast and easy all of these techniques are, once you know the tricks to them.

And have you heard? There's been a veritable explosion of new and amazing threads available to quilters. Once you get to know and love them, you will wonder how you ever survived without them. Of course, the key to thread is to understand it—the old one-size-fits-any-purpose days have gone. We'll explore thread in all its glory, up to and including how to design your own fabric with it.

Kids have play dates—you should, too! As you browse through *Quilt Toppings*, invite your friends over to look at the photos, share ideas, laugh, then try something new. What could be more fun?

Garden Windows, Bendigo.
See page 36.

Xishaungbanna (shee-shaung-banna), Melody Crust, 56" × 71." The red parasol is painted with paint sticks. Although they appear to be appliqued, the yellow flowers are actually the result of stenciling! I cut the flower shapes out of freezer paper, laid them on top of the parasol stencil, and painted over the top of both. The yellow showing through is actually the yellow fabric of the pieced quilt top.

1 PAINTS, CRAYONS, INKS, FOIL, AND MORE

The **JOY** of painting, drawing, foiling, or using other embellishment techniques directly onto fabric is that there are so many **POSSIBILITIES** and so few rules. This is a time to set free your imagination, pick up brush, paint sticks, crayons, or stamps and **PLAY**. How do you decide what works well or what doesn't? By applying the same **TECHNIQUES** you use to create a quilt top, of course,—visual trial and error. Not only can you **EMBELLISH** your fabrics before you put them into a quilt, but you can paint, draw, stamp, or foil onto the quilt at any stage of its development. Play with fabric paints to **ENRICH** your fabrics before you begin sewing—or at any time during the process. Use acrylic paints, paint sticks, or even crayons to add new designs or **DIMENSION** to portions of your quilts, making the fabrics uniquely your own. Add spectacular metallic **HIGHLIGHTS** with custom foiling. Or simply use inks or marking pens to draw unusual designs onto your quilt top. The choices are yours and the **MAGIC** is waiting to happen.

PAINT, GLORIOUS PAINT

Once you begin working with acrylic paints, fabric paints, or spray paints, you will quickly find that there need be no rules to the creative process. Paint onto any natural fiber, including cottons, muslin, silk, and rayon, but don't stop there. Tone-on-tone fabrics are fun to paint with transparent acrylics or fabric paint, because the print shows through to the surface. Try this with small-scale geometrics, for instance—the results are often delightful. You might even try painting on the back side of the fabric, if the notion of a subtler design appeals to you. You may paint the fabrics before you piece them into a quilt—or you can wait until the piecing or appliqué is complete. Painting an otherwise "finished" quilt top allows you to highlight portions that please you. You might decide to personalize a child's quilt by carefully imposing the child's handprint onto the surface. Or you might boldly swoop a colorful design across multiple blocks of a pieced quilt. In any case, be prepared for the wonderful special effects that follow when you pick up your paints.

Prep Work and Supplies

Natural fabrics, such as cotton, work best for most paint. Pre-wash the fabric if it has a lot of sizing in it or if you think you may want to wash the finished quilt. I suggest you use Synthrapol, a commercially produced fabric wash. Avoid using fabric softener or dryer sheets as these can leave a residue that will prevent the paint

Nighttime, Melody Crust, 4" × 6." All color, except the stitching and binding, is applied with paint sticks and shows up very well on the dark background fabric of this mini quilt.

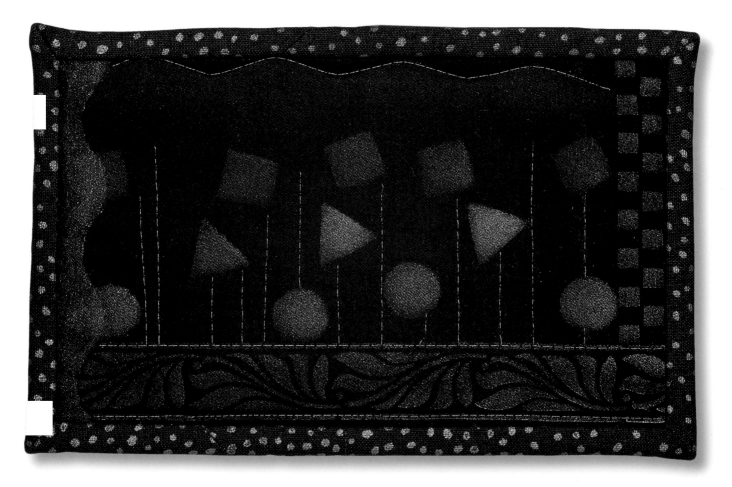

Abstract, *Melody Crust, 4" × 6."*
Positive stencil shapes and freezer
paper cut with a decorative cutter
are the basis of this totally painted
composition.

from adhering properly. As an alternative, you can also use prepared-for-dying (PFD) material, which is already washed and free of sizing or other chemicals.

With fabric paints, you can paint when the fabric is wet or dry. If you want a multi-colored design, let the paint dry between each color. For a blended effect, mix paints right on the fabric, applying one color over another while the paint is still wet. Color blending is much easier to achieve with wet fabric, so use either a spray bottle or paint brush to dampen it.

Unlike dye, which bonds chemically with the fabric, paint simply sits on top of the fibers. The type of paint you use and how it is applied will determine the "hand" or stiffness, of the finished product. A soft hand means there is no apparent change to the fabric, while a hard hand means that you feel mostly paint, not fabric. The nature of your project and how much hand you prefer will help you decide which kind of paint to choose.

Below left, ***Benjamin Bunny***, *Christine Palmer, painted by Karen Morgan, quilted by Sue Theiler, 42" × 58." These darling hand-painted bunnies were done freehand.* Below Right, ***Benjamin Bunny***, *detail. Notice how embroidery is used to enhance the overall effect.*

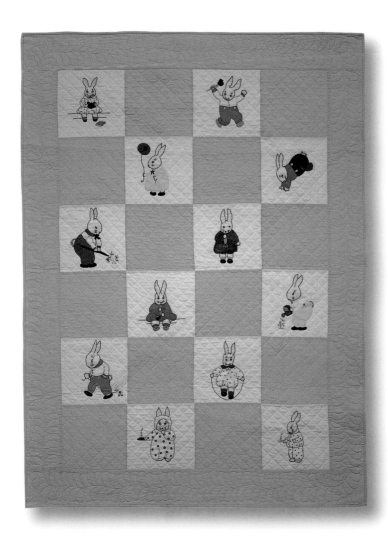

Stabilize!

It always helps to stabilize your fabric before you begin to paint. I use freezer paper for this purpose. The freezer paper adheres to the fabric in a temporary bonding process that helps hold the fabric steady and wrinkle-free while you paint or draw on it. Cut a piece of freezer paper larger than the project you are working on. Place the plastic-coated side of the paper against the wrong side of the fabric. Use a dry iron at a cotton setting to adhere the paper to the fabric. The plastic won't hurt the material and the whole thing peels off easily when you are finished.

Acrylic Craft Paints

Acrylic craft paints are wonderful on quilt tops. Inexpensive and easy to use, they come in a multitude of colors, including metallics and iridescents. They can be used straight from the jar or bottle, and can be thinned to any consistency. The different brands of paint vary greatly in thickness. The thicker the paint, the heavier the hand it makes.

In general, thicker paints are excellent choices for stenciling, for painting directly onto fabric, and for stamping. You can also use them to attach beads or buttons. Sprinkling wet paint with glitter is another fun effect. If you want a softer hand, you can easily thin acrylic paint with water. You can also thin acrylic paints with *fabric*

Even very dark fabrics can be beautifully enhanced with opaque paint. This space theme was painted with acrylic paint using a purchased stencil.

SUPPLIES CHECKLIST

Most of the supplies you'll need for painting are already available in your kitchen or workroom. Others are waiting for you at your local fabric shop or art supply store.

✓ **PAINT** Choose acrylic craft paints, fabric paints, or spray paints. If you are using spray paints, the only other supplies you need are for clean-up!

✓ **WATER** to dilute paints—and for clean-up

✓ **PALETTE, PAPER PLATE, OR PAINT-MIXING TRAY** An old ice cube tray is ideal for mixing paints

✓ **BRUSHES** in a variety of sizes and types

✓ **PAPER TOWELS** for clean-up

✓ **PLASTIC SHEET** to cover work surface

✓ **FREEZER PAPER**

Optional

• Fabric medium to dilute acrylic paints

• Stamps, including commercial rubber stamps and "found" objects

• Stencils, sponges, gloves

ABOVE RIGHT, *Many different paint applicators are available. These examples are (left to right) a sea sponge, brayer, foam brush, paint brushes, and stencil brushes.* BELOW RIGHT, *There are a wide variety of paints available for a quilter's use. Shown here are some of the acrylic, fabric, craft and spray paints you can use on fabric.*

medium, available in craft and quilt stores. This specialty thinner seems to make the paint more fabric-friendly.

Don't hesitate to combine different brands of acrylic paint. I've mixed and matched brands many times and they work together beautifully.

Heat-Setting

Once you have finished painting, you will need to *heat-set* your work. It's important to heat-set all painted designs in order to lock the color onto the fibers and allow for future cleaning. Let craft paints cure for at least 24 hours before heat-setting. This will add to the paint's durability. Set an iron to the maximum temperature allowable for your fabric. Put a piece of aluminum foil on your ironing board, then set the fabric on top of it, painted side down, and press for 15 to 20 seconds. It's as simple as that!

Fabric Paints

Fabric paints are made especially for use on fabric and hold up well to repeated washing, making them the better choice for clothing or a quilt you are going to want to toss into the washing machine. The three most common categories are transparent paints, opaque paints, and metallics. If you wish, you can mix the types together for different results.

Painted Desert, Melody Crust, 40" × 48." I wanted an off-grain pink and blue checkerboard fabric for the border. Hunting high and low produced nothing but frustration, so I sat down and painted my own with fabric paint.

Transfer Magic

No matter the medium you are using (paints, crayons, inks, foils, or other), you may sometimes wish to transfer a particular pattern onto your fabric. To transfer patterns onto light fabric, trace the design onto the matte side of a piece of freezer paper using a dark permanent marker. Don't mark on the shiny plastic side because the ink might inadvertently rub off. Iron the freezer paper to the back of the fabric and the dark lines will show through, making it very easy to trace.

For dark or opaque fabric, begin by tracing the pattern onto a sheet of tracing paper. Next, lay your fabric on the work surface and place a sheet of quilter's transfer paper (a type of carbon paper made especially for sewing purposes) over it. Put the traced pattern, penciled side down, on top. With a ballpoint pen, go over all the traced lines of the design, pressing firmly. The pattern is now on your fabric. One more tip—yellow transfer paper works well with dark materials.

Fabric from the thirties provided the makings for a friendship block, which was painted rather than pieced.

Transparent paint adds color over the top of the fabric. You can still see the pattern and texture of the material, but there is now an exciting new design adding extra interest. These paints leave the fabric with a soft hand. Brand names to look for include Jacquard Dye-Na-Flow™, Textile™ (semi-transparent), Pebeo Setacolor™, Setsasilk™, and PROchem PRO® Fab Textile (semi-transparent) paints. All blend well on the fabric and on your palette.

Opaque paints cover very well and are the only option for solid coverage on a black or very dark fabric. Opaque paints are great to use for almost any application. They are thick in the jar and leave a heavy hand on the fabric. The colors tend to be bold. They can be easily mixed on the palette but will resist running together during direct application onto fabric.

Metallic paints leave a very heavy hand. They work best when heavily diluted or used for highlights.

To make paint easier to spread, try diluting it with anywhere from 25 percent to 50 percent water. Just keep in mind that full-strength paint will be intense, and the more you dilute it, the lighter the color will be. Diluted paint doesn't store particularly well, so plan to use it up in a few days. Consider left-over paints an opportunity to try something new—experiment with them.

Heat-Setting

To heat-set fabric paint, let your work cure for at least 24 hours. Press with a hot iron (or as hot as the fabric allows) for 20 seconds on each side. You may also put the fabric in a hot dryer for 30 minutes.

Paint, ink, or permanent marker pens can dramatically change store-bought fabrics either before or after they are pieced and/or appliquéd.

Highlighting

Use a small, pointed craft or artist brush to add depth to a design by outlining something you have already painted or a detail in a particular fabric. When you outline, you make the design really pop. For instance, you might choose to outline a yellow flower with black paint or put shiny gold around a red design.

Different effects are possible with different types of brushes, too. Compare the results when you use a fan-shaped brush rather than a flat-tip brush. Experiment with dots, curves, arrows, squiggles, and straight lines. You can also *overpaint* on top of an intricate design. Highlighting is a wonderful place to let loose your creative instincts—the choices are all your own.

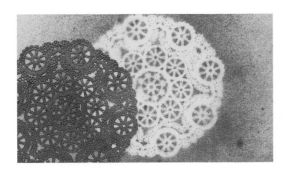

A paper doily is a good mask (or resist) to use with spray paints, especially if your project calls for a more formal design. You could cut your doily into wedges to make very delicate fan shapes.

Spray Paints

A variety of paints is available in aerosol or pump bottles. They are generally permanent and washable. Some have an airbrush effect; while others add extra sparkle. Before you begin working with spray paints, I recommend finding a large cardboard box that you can use as a spray booth—this will alleviate fears of unintentionally painting either yourself or your house!

Painting Yardage

You can paint yardage before incorporating it into a quilt using acrylics, fabric paints, spray paints, or Setacolor Transparent paints. There are a variety of ways to work. Use a flat-end brush either to spread paint evenly over the surface or to dab it on, creating a mottled look. This is also a good brush to freehand stripes or lines. Alternatively, use a regular household brush to make large-scale brush strokes. Consider adding a toothbrush to your brush collection. It will be great for spattering and rubbing paint into your fabric.

Sponges, either natural or man-made, can be used to dab paint onto fabric or to add more colors to an already painted area. Use them either wet or dry to create different looks. You can also scrunch up plastic wrap and use it to dab paint onto the

To paint checkerboard fabric pink and blue, I used a fat Sharpie pen and drew a 2" grid on freezer paper. Because I wanted the print to be off-grain, I was careful to position the fabric off kilter on the grid-lined paper. Using the grid as reference (the fat ink lines made it visible through my fabric), I ironed 2" squares of freezer paper onto the right side of the fabric and painted the exposed parts pink. After the paint dried, I moved the squares to cover the pink and painted with blue paint. Cutting the fabric on-grain makes the sewing much easier and ultimately resulted in a design that appears off-grain. Just the look I wanted!

FABRIC PAINTS

Brand Name	Use for	Finish	Washability	Toxicity	Hand	Heat Set	Clean up	Notes
Jacquard Lumiere	Stamping, stenciling, hand-painting	Very metallic	Machine wash or dry clean		Heavy	Iron	Water	Mixes with all Jacquard lines; Add up to 25 percent water to lighten colors
Jacquard Neopaque	Stamping, stenciling, hand-painting	Opaque	Machine wash		Soft	Iron	Soap and water	Covers dark fabrics well
Pebeo Setacolor	Sun painting, hand-painting	Transparent	Hand or machine wash; dry clean		Soft	Iron or oven	Soap and water	30 colors available; 10 available in aerosol cans
Jacquard Textile Colors	Hand-painting, printing	Semi-transparent	Machine wash; dry clean	None	Soft	Iron	Soap and water	Non-fading, lightfast
Spray Art	Air brush effect		Hand wash	None	Soft	No	Soap and water	Available in aerosol can
Tulip Fabric Glitter	Adding sparkle	Glitter	Machine wash, line dry	Not for hair or skin	Soft	No	Soap and water	Comes in spray bottle
Delta Color Mist	Spraying on fabric	Transparent	Machine wash (test for best results)	None	Soft	Iron	Cold water	Resulting paint color is affected by fabric color

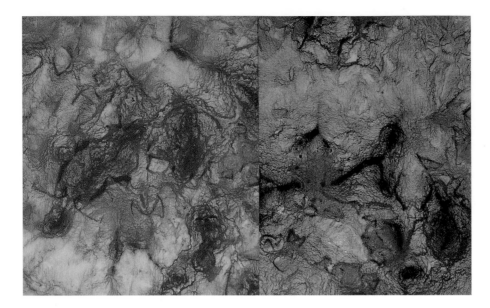

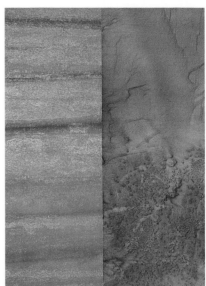

ABOVE LEFT, *Painting damp fabric with runny paint and bunching it to dry can create an infinite variety of patterns. On the left is fabric painted with red fabric paint; on the right is the same red paint with blue dabbed onto the high spots.* ABOVE RIGHT, *The pink stripes were painted with runny paint and folded to dry. The bottom half of the blue fabric was sprinkled with salt.*

fabric. Almost any painting technique that you can apply to a wall can be applied with equal success to fabric.

Any number of methods will give you a unique and interesting result. Try painting a fat quarter all over with rather runny fabric paint, then scrunch the fabric up. You will find that the scrunched fabric wants to relax before it has dried, but you can fix this easily by pushing the wadded up fabric into a small, lidless plastic container until it dries. The paint will dry unevenly—it will be darker in the valleys, lighter at the peaks. Another idea is to paint and scrunch the fabric, then, while it is still in the container, hit just the high points with another color or two. This is particularly effective if you use a metallic paint (just remember, a little goes a long

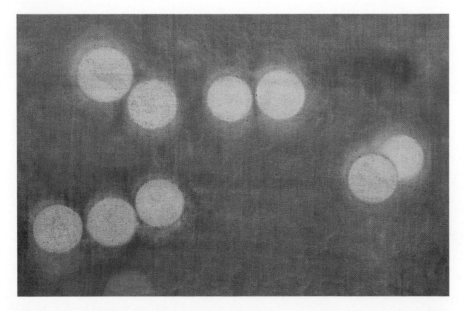

Sun printing using dimes and pennies as the resists.

Sun Printing

Sun printing is easy and fun, making it a good technique to try out with children. Dilute Setacolor Transparent paints using three parts water to one part paint. Apply the paint, then arrange any objects—or *resists*—you choose, such as leaves, fern fronds, coins, paint brushes, or almost anything with distinct edges, on top of the fabric. Leave the fabric out in the sun until it is completely dry then lift off the resists. The parts shaded from the sun dry lighter.

way). For a completely different look, paint the fabric then accordion-pleat it. I use wooden clothes pins to hold it in position for drying.

Another easy technique involves scattering salt over the wet fabric paint. When the paint dries, gently brush the salt off. You will have an interesting mottled design.

A great tool—the *brayer*—allows you to spread very thin layers of paint onto fabric (a brayer also works well with inks, which are discussed later in this chapter). Soft rubber brayers come in a variety of sizes and are readily available in art and craft supply stores. Mix paint to the consistency of heavy cream, then pour about a half teaspoon onto a piece of aluminum foil (to allow for easy clean up). Roll the brayer until it is evenly coated with paint. Rolling the brayer forward applies the paint and going backwards rolls it off. It's fun to experiment with a brayer to create special effects. Try putting rubber bands around the roller and see what happens. Or arrange strings or other items beneath the fabric then roll over them with the paint-covered brayer.

A brayer with a light coating of paint rolled over a purchased stamp or one you make yourself adds interesting texture. The home made stamp shown here is a small block of wood wrapped with heavy twine.

Stamping with Paints

Almost anything can be used as a stamp. A kitchen utensil, such as a potato masher, can make an interesting pattern. Personalize a quilt by using children's footprints. Let nature inspire you and use flat flowers and leaves for the unique imprints they lend to your work. Pencil erasers make nice dots, eyes, or noses; cotton swabs make dots with softer edges. A cosmetic sponge makes a great stamp, and it's easy to cut a compressed sponge into any shape you like. And speaking of cutting things to any shape, both linoleum flooring blocks and gum erasers offer the opportunity to easily carve your own permanent stamps. There is a wealth of found objects

LEFT, **Soles**, *Heather Waldron, 57" × 86." Heather used fabric paint and her clever version of the ultimate rubber stamp—tennis shoes!* ABOVE, **Soles**, *detail. The spatter painting, done with a regular paintbrush, adds interest to the background.*

all around you! Heavy twine wrapped around a block of wood or washers glued to a wooden block both work well. Look at everyday objects with stamping in mind and you will be amazed at the myriad possibilities.

Prepare your fabric just as you would for any other form of painting (see pages 6–8). You may already have commercially made stamps on hand. If the designs are right for your project, by all means use them, just

These rubber stamps are (left to right) off-the-shelf, an easy-to-cut sponge that swells when wet, and a linoleum block that I shape with a cutter set intended for block printing.

rough up the surface first with fine sandpaper to ensure better paint application. If not, you certainly don't have to rush out and buy some. You can easily make your own stamps using a potato and a cookie cutter. Just cut a raw potato in half lengthwise, push a cookie cutter all the way through one of the halves and cut off or break away any excess potato left outside of the cutter. Push the potato design out of the cookie cutter and blot the flat side of your new stamp on a paper towel. You can use your potato stamp many times for each stamping session and then throw it out. If you need the same design at a later time, just make a new one.

You will have better control of the amount of paint you are applying if you brush paint onto your stamp rather than dipping the stamp into a dish of paint. I find that I get better results when I use the paint sparingly. So, paint your stamp, slap it onto your fabric, press down firmly, and gently pull it straight up. Don't slide your stamp off, as this will blur the image. If the paint isn't perfectly applied you can always touch it up with a small brush. Before you do this, though, step back and take a look at your work. Sometimes the little imperfections are what make your stampings charming and unique.

PAINT STICKS

Easy to use, paint sticks are shaped like oversized crayons and have about the same consistency. Amazingly, they can replicate the look of *air brushing*, without your having to invest in or bother with special equipment. Paint sticks applied to silk or cotton are simple, fun, and permanent and they leave a very soft hand.

Pears, *Kay Taylor, 22″ × 20.″ Kay does a wonderful job of demonstrating the delicacy that can be achieved using paint sticks on both the pears and the diamond shapes.*

Prep Work and Supplies

As with other painting materials, cover your work surface with paper to catch any mess before you get started. Pre-wash and press the fabric. You might want to take the time to iron your fabric to some freezer paper, because this will make it more cooperative when you start to paint on it.

I always have success with Shiva brand paint sticks and use them exclusively. They are available in both "mini stick" sets and artist sizes, in a wide range of colors with finishes from matte to iridescent. Whichever brand you choose, be sure to follow the manufacturer's instructions. Always make a test sample and launder it so there are no surprises.

Working with Paint Sticks

Remove the self-healing protective coating of paint from the flat end of your paint stick with an X-acto knife. If you are stencilling, use masking tape to hold your stencil in place and to protect any areas you don't want to color. Rub the paint stick with a stencil brush and dab the brush onto a paper towel to remove any excess paint. This is definitely a time where more isn't better, so don't overload your brush with paint. You can always add another layer or two. Using firm, short

*ABOVE, **Imperial Flowers**, Melody Crust, 24" × 36." Red paint stick applied over a variety of fabrics, including cotton and silk. ABOVE LEFT, **Imperial Flowers**, detail. Red paint stick over a metallic fabric allows the metallic threads to shine through.*

SUPPLIES CHECKLIST

A few inexpensive supplies and you are ready to go.

- ✓ **PAINT STICKS** Follow manufacturer's directions
- ✓ **STENCIL BRUSHES**
- ✓ **X-ACTO KNIFE**
- ✓ **PAPER PLATE**
- ✓ **BABY WIPES** or odorless mineral spirits for clean up
- ✓ **PAPER TOWELS** for clean-up
- ✓ **PLASTIC SHEET** to cover work surface

Optional
- • Gloves
- • Stencils

A variety of paint sticks. Once you start to use them, you will find your collection of colors grows by leaps and bounds.

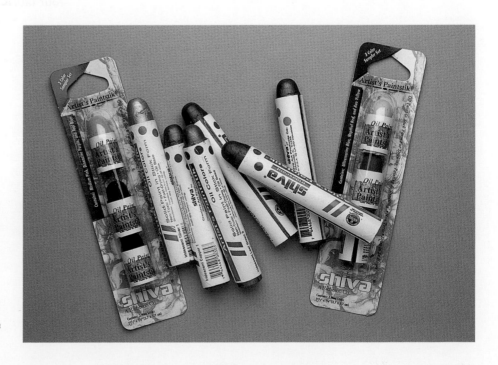

strokes, apply the paint in one direction. Start at the outer edges and work inward. When you are satisfied, pull off your stencil and take off any extra masking tape.

Instead of using a brush, paint sticks can be applied directly to fabric, just as you would use a crayon. Keep in mind, though, that this method gives you less control over the paint. It's also fun to place rubber stamps—or anything with an interesting texture—under the fabric and rub the paint stick lightly over it. Whenever you use this rubbing technique, skip the step of applying a freezer paper backing to your fabric.

Clean up your tools immediately; baby wipes, believe it or not, work best. If a couple of hours or more has passed (life happens!) and the paint is dry or nearly so, use odorless mineral spirits to clean up. Any bits of loose paint come right off with a lint roller or a few pieces of masking tape.

Heat-Setting

Allow your work to cure at least 24 hours before heat-setting it. Set a dry iron to the wool setting, approximately 300°F, and put a press cloth or a clean scrap of paper over your work, both to prevent your iron from coming into direct contact with the paint and to absorb any excess paint. Working on a firm surface, iron smoothly for about 10 seconds, using light, even pressure. Make sure that all areas of the design come in contact with the heat.

Cape Cod Cherries, *detail. Quilter Christine Palmer used crayons to create these luscious cherries. See full quilt on page 34.*

CRAYONS

Crayons on fabric can give the beautiful effect of a watercolor painting. Darker colored crayons seem to work best, but a shaded fabric or a "white on cream" can also add a subtle yet wonderful element. Because of the delicacy of the finished work, crayons are usually paired with outline embroidery. The texture of the fabric and the crayon strokes will both show. Colorings that have great depth and beauty are usually the result of layering the colors, so you will probably find you are most successful when you apply many soft layers. The more layers you apply, the more depth to your coloring.

Prep Work

Regular crayons generally work well on natural fabrics. They come in a huge variety of colors and are made by many different manufacturers. The more color and the less wax in the crayon, the better the results, so I suggest you buy a good quality crayon made by a name you recognize.

Cape Cod Cherries, *detail. The cherries are colored with many light layers of crayon, making the image both even and bold.*

Fabric crayons are ideal for transferring colorful designs permanently to synthetic blend fabrics.

Begin by ironing the fabric to freezer paper in order to temporarily stabilize it while you are coloring. You might also want to make a freezer paper stencil to help you "stay within the lines." Practice coloring on scraps of material so you can decide what technique yields the optimal result. Coloring with the blunt end of the crayon works best and slightly rounding off the sharp edges makes it easier to use. Work in one small area at a time because it's difficult to apply crayon evenly over very large spaces.

Start lightly—remember, you can always add more. Work from the outside in and keep the strokes of any single layer going in one direction. Areas can be made darker later by adding additional layers and stroking in another direction.

Use an iron to press each layer of crayon separately. Put your work face down on a clean cloth or paper towel, cover with another cloth or paper towel to keep your iron clean, and press with a medium hot iron for several seconds. Much of the wax can be removed if you use freezer paper in place of a press cloth. The waxy side needs to face the crayoned area.

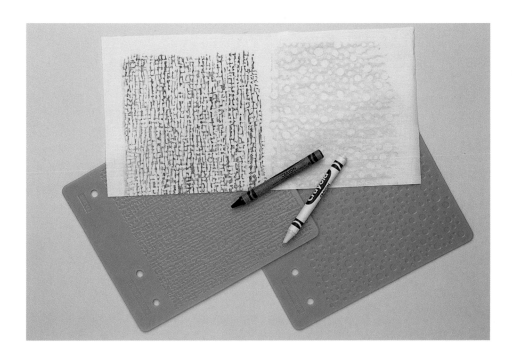

Rubbing crayons or paint sticks over different textures creates wonderful fabric. Shown here are texture plates (available in craft and scrapbooking stores) generally used for paper.

Crayon Rubbings

Crayons and rubbing are a great combination of medium and technique. Have you bought potatoes in a mesh bag lately? How about berries in a plastic basket? Do you have any rough-surfaced tiles or pieces of slate left over from a patio project? Interesting rubber stamps? All of these and many other common household objects make fabulous textures if you lay them under your fabric and gently rub a crayon over the top. For obvious reasons, rubbing always works best when you skip the freezer paper backing.

MARKING PENS

For any fine-line work or for outlining, there is no better tool than a marking pen. Comfortable to use and requiring little or no preparation or clean up, markers can add a variety of special effects to your work.

Baltimore Revisited, *Melody Crust, 12″ × 12.″ My quick version of a Baltimore Album quilt is inked. After making a paper pattern, I placed it on a light-table. Fabric ironed to freezer paper was set on top and the design was copied onto it with permanent fabric pens. Everything except the inner border and the binding was drawn with ink.*

Prep Work and Supplies

Choosing 100 percent cottons will give you great results because there is much less bleeding than with polyester fabrics. A bit of practice on a scrap of material will tell you what speed it's best to use in writing on your particular fabric. Some inks will bleed if you write too slowly and some fabrics take a little time to absorb the ink and won't let you write too fast. This isn't difficult at all, it just warrants a bit of practice to determine how to get the best results from your particular combination of ink and fabric. It's a good idea to test your scrap for bleeding and washability before you actually mark your project. Prepare your fabric in the same way you would for painting (see pages 6–8). Pre-wash it without softeners or dryer sheets and stabilize it by applying a temporary freezer paper backing.

Quilting stencils work very well for painting fabric. On the left is the difference a fabric marker can make to plain white fabric. On the right, a rubber stamp image was added to jazz up the design even more.

Marking pens come in myriad colors and sizes and are available at your local quilt shop, art supply, scrapbooking or stationery store, or through specialty catalogs. Be sure to look for pens with ink that is permanent and acid free. Pens come in a variety of sizes, usually from 0.005 to 0.1—the lower the number, the smaller the point. Fine-point permanent fabric marking pens are colorfast and resist bleeding. Pigma Micron® pens are a good choice. Remember that no matter what type of marking pen you choose, it will keep much, much longer if you always keep the cap on tight every time you set it down.

Lettering with Markers

If you are lettering, start by making a pattern on lined paper. The lines help keep your lettering straight. Position the letters and figures exactly as you want them to appear on your project. (A word to the wise—avoid disaster by double checking your spelling.) If there is a particular design you want to use, copy it onto a piece of plain paper. Use masking tape to secure your stabilized fabric over the pattern you have already taped onto your window or light table and trace directly onto your material, using whatever color marking pen you choose.

I use the special fonts in my computer for the lettering patterns. That way, I can choose the size and style with the push of a button, with the added bonus of spell check!

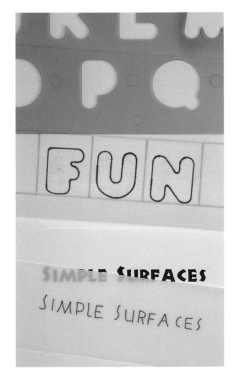

Stenciling and tracing are two effective ways to write on fabric. To keep stenciled letters evenly spaced, draw bold guidelines with a fat Sharpie pen directly onto the freezer paper. For tracing, make a paper pattern either on lined paper or with a computer printer. Stabilize the fabric with freezer paper and trace. A light table makes this job a snap!

This simple flower is colored with bottled fabric inks applied with an ink applicator. I lightly drew the design with a pencil. The inks, when wet, blend easily, which automatically creates the shading. Matching colored ink pens from the same company add extra detail.

Freehand Designs

Marking pens are a wonderful tool for making freehand designs. Use them to add details such as veins on leaves or shading on flower petals. Whimsical creatures, perhaps a fairy or a frog peeping out from behind a flower, can add a delightful personal touch.

Heat-Setting

When you have finished marking, let the ink cure for 24 hours, then heat-set it with the warmest iron your fabric allows for 15 to 20 seconds and remove the freezer paper backing.

ALL-PURPOSE INKS

When you think about ink, don't limit yourself to just schoolhouse black. There are many different colors of inks, pens, and stamp pads available and you can mix and match them with abandon. You can even find white ink, which is perfect for highlighting or blending. Un-inked, disposable or reusable applicators are available with either brush or bullet tips. You can also apply inks with a cosmetic sponge or small paintbrush to create a different texture.

LABEL IT!

Marking pens are a terrific tool for making labels for your projects. All of the hours of creativity and effort that you have put into it need to be recognized. Have you ever seen or owned an old quilt that is anonymous? Wouldn't you love to know where and when it was made, and by whom? Someday, someone will feel exactly the same about your quilts, so by all means, label them!

MARKERS

Type	Line	Heat-Set	Washability	Toxicity	Colors	Clean up	Notes
Tsukineko Fabrico Markers	Bullet and brush	Not required but recommended	Machine wash	None, acid free	Pastel, landscape, standard, sorbet sets available	Soap and water	Fade resistant, store horizontally
Sakura® Micron Pigma Pens	Varies	Iron	Machine wash	None, acid free	Many	Soap and water	Will not fade
Marvy Fabric Marker	3mm	Not required	Machine wash or dry clean	None	Standard, fluorescent	Soap and water	
Deco Fabric	3mm	Iron	Machine wash	None, acid free	Metallic, opaque	Soap and water while still wet	Covers dark fabrics
Fabric Mate Permanent Super Fine	Varies	Not required	Machine wash	None, acid free	Standard, fluorescent, pastels	Soap and water	Colors mix together

INKS

Brand Name	Use for	Finish	Washability	Toxicity	Hand	Heat-Set	Clean up	Notes
Tsukineko	Stamping, stenciling, hand-painting	Opaque, transparent, metallic	Machine wash	None	Soft	Iron or dryer	Water	Available in stamp pads, too

If you like the idea of using ink to achieve a watercolor look, you can mix up to three parts of ink with one part water. Experiment a bit to find the right mix for you.

Prep Work and Supplies

Tsukineko all-purpose ink has the consistency of water with the added bonus that it's available in bottles, stamp pads, and markers. The inks come with applicators that are a cross between a pen and a brush and are as easy to control as a marker while less intimidating than a brush.

As with all these surface finishes, prepare your fabric by pre-washing it without softeners or dryer sheets. I find it usually isn't necessary to stabilize fabric before inking if I am working in a small area, and that it's helpful to work on a disposable, padded surface, such as a few layers of paper towel.

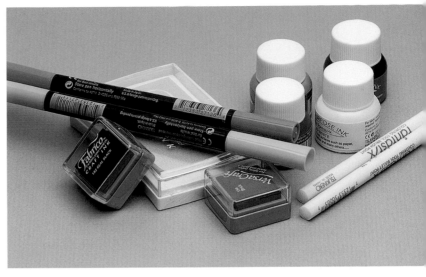

All-purpose inks are available in many colors and forms. It's fun to mix and match them and to experiment with the different applicators.

Heat-Setting

To heat-set inks, press the inked fabric with the hottest iron allowed for the fabric. I recommend ironing on a piece of aluminum foil for about 10 to 15 seconds. You can also tumble the fabric in a hot dryer for 30 seconds. (Yes, that's *seconds*, not minutes as you would for paint.)

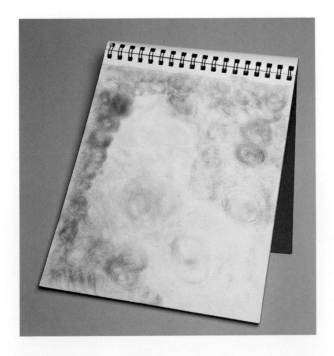

Keep a Sketchbook

Keep a drawing tablet or sketchbook close at hand and wipe your paint-laden brushes on it before cleaning them. The result will be a collection of pretty papers to use as unique greeting cards or wrapping paper.

Or, give a completed notebook to a child and he or she will find plenty of uses for it.

Galaxy, Melody Crust, 24″ × 36.″ The opulence of foil adds richness to these simple pieced blocks. It was very simple to fasten freezer paper stencils to the fabric, apply glue, and iron on the different colors of foil.

FOILING

Bring your projects to life with instant glitz and shine. Foiling on fabric is easy, fun, and permanent. You can apply foil directly to the fabric or onto an area you have already painted. This material works very well on raised, or "puffy," paints. Foil usually comes in sheets and is available in any number of wonderful colors. You will notice that each sheet is shiny on one side and a bit dull on the other. The dull side is the foil, while the shiny side is the plastic backing that you will eventually peel away.

Prep Work and Supplies

For foiling, your fabric will need to be clean and perfectly flat, so pre-wash and iron it before you begin. The idea is to get the foil off the plastic film and onto the fabric, so *always* put the colored side up and facing you! You will have better control of the process if you work in one small area at a time. In any case, always test first to make sure you are going to get the results you expect.

Getting Ready for Foil

As with paint, freezer paper can be used as an iron-on stencil. You can cut a positive image and apply your adhesive outside the blocked space. Alternatively, cut out the shape you want, remove it, and use the negative space inside to guide your adhesive application. For an unusual effect, you can cut out your stencil with decorative scis-

SUPPLIES CHECKLIST

Foil is easy to apply and there are few items needed.

✓ **COLORED FOIL**

✓ **ADHESIVE**

✓ **APPLICATOR** such as sponge, foam brush, or toothbrush

✓ **PAPER SCISSORS, FABRIC SCISSORS**

✓ **MASKING TAPE**

✓ **PAPER TOWEL OR RAG,** soap and water for clean up

Optional

• Stencils

• Burnishing tools

• Rubber stamps

Be sure to have the shiny, colored side up in all foil applications!

sors or tear the freezer paper for a feathered edge look. If a freezer paper stencil is impractical for the spaces you want to foil, use masking tape to create either positive or negative shapes.

If you are using a pre-made stencil, just apply the adhesive in the area to be foiled with a brush or sponge.

Using rubber stamps is another good way to apply adhesive for foiling. Apply glue to the stamp with an up-and-down "pouncing" motion, set the stamp straight down onto your fabric without rocking it, then lift it straight off. Some adhesives will destroy rubber stamps, so be sure to wash them immediately with soap and water.

Silk screening is another possibility, just be sure you don't let the adhesive dry in your screens because it will be there forever! As soon as possible, wash your screens thoroughly and wipe them dry.

Foil Adhesives

The foil is as permanent as the adhesive you choose. In general, the less glue you use, the better. You can apply the glue with a toothbrush, sea sponge, your finger, or a stamp. Let the glue dry completely before applying the foil. Some glues will be tacky when dry; the manufacturer's package will tell you how long you should wait before you apply the foil. Liquid adhesive lets you draw your design directly onto your material. Flexible glues work well on stretchable fabric. If you are working on a fabric that you know is completely non-washable, you can even foil using double-sided tape!

Burnishing

Burnishing is a simple, hands-on way to apply foil. Iron the fabric to some freezer paper or lay it on a piece of newspaper. Screen, stamp, or draw with glue the shape you want onto your fabric and let it dry. Carefully place the foil sheet, colored side up and facing you, onto your material. Scrape with your fingernail, a paperclip, or other burnishing tool in order to adhere the foil to the fabric. This will also separate the foil from its plastic backing. Peel away the plastic sheet, leaving the foil stuck only to the areas where you have applied your adhesive.

Halo, *Melody Crust, 12" × 16." Freezer paper stencils were ironed onto the fabric. Glue was then applied and different colors of foil were heat-set using an iron.*

RIGHT, **Cosmic Dream**, Melody Crust, 24" × 36." This whole-cloth quilt started as a half yard of plain white fabric. I painted the dampened fabric with various shades of blue fabric paint, let it dry thoroughly, and then heat-set the foil stars. ABOVE, **Cosmic Dream**, detail. Not following the rules and removing the foil immediately allows for partial coverage the first time. A second application of yellow foil adds depth.

Another option is iron-on fusible web. Just remember that a fusible web may have a texture that will leave its own impression. Cut the shapes you want from a piece of web, place it on your fabric, and iron it as described below.

Applying Foil with Heat

Either iron your fabric onto freezer paper or lay it on a piece of newspaper. Screen, stamp, or draw the glue onto it in whatever shape or design you want. Let the glue dry to a very slightly tacky state (a hair dryer may speed this process). On a firm ironing surface, carefully position the foil sheet, colored side up and facing you, onto the fabric. Set a dry iron on a wool setting, about 300°F. Place a press cloth over the foil to prevent the iron from coming in direct contact with it because ironing directly on the foil will damage both it and the adhesive. Iron for ten seconds using small, circular motions, making sure that all areas of the design come in contact with the heat.

For fuller coverage, allow your work to cool completely, then gently peel away the plastic sheet. The foil will stick only to the areas where the adhesive has been applied. For less concentration of foil, remove while still warm.

In an area where foiling is sparse, a second color can be applied. Foil will adhere as long as there is glue still exposed and available. When applying one foil over another, you need to lower your iron heat to a silk-nylon setting, or about 225°F.

STENCILING

Stenciling is a wonderfully easy way to transfer even the most intricate of designs onto fabric. Unlike freehand work, you don't need to have a steady hand—the stencil does most of the work for you.

For instant gratification, a huge variety of pre-cut stencils are available at quilt and craft shops. Just tape one to your fabric and get started! If you prefer, you can

BELOW LEFT, **Sweet Potato Vine**, *Melody Crust, 36" × 47." Two off-the-shelf stencils along with green, yellow, and gold paint sticks made all of these blocks. Thanks to the paint sticks, they look as if they have been air brushed.* BELOW RIGHT, **Sweet Potato Vine**, *detail. One ivy stencil, just as it came from the store.* BOTTOM RIGHT, **Sweet Potato Vine**, *detail. The flower is a combination of shapes from one stencil, with masking tape blocking out the unwanted parts.*

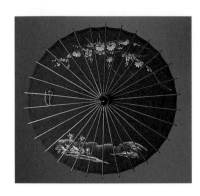

This photo was the pattern for **Xishaungbanna** *on page 4. First I projected the slide onto the pieced background to audition it for placement. Without moving the projector, I replaced my quilt top with freezer paper (paper side facing me) and traced the outline. After cutting out the design, I ironed the newly made stencil to the fabric, placed some cut out flower stencils in a pleasing arrangement, and painted over the top with paint sticks.*

cut your own stencil from plastic, freezer paper, or stiff cardboard. A manila folder works well—and you can extend its life by sealing it with a clear acrylic spray. Freezer paper stencils don't last long but they are easy to cut and have an added benefit—because the paper is temporarily bonded to the fabric, nothing will leak under the stencil. With the help of a light box or brightly lit window, trace or free-hand draw the design directly onto your stencil material, then cut it out with an X-acto knife.

You can either cut out a *positive* or a *negative* version of the design. For a positive version, simply cut out the shape, lay it on the fabric, and apply color *outside* the blocked space. For a negative impression, cut out the shape, discard it, then color the negative area—that is, the area *inside* the cutout. Remember, too, that straight scissors aren't the only choice when it comes to cutting. Try using decorative scissors for added effect.

Smooth-woven natural fabrics work best for stenciling. Pre-wash your fabric without softeners or dryer sheets and stabilize it by applying a temporary freezer paper backing, just as you would prepare it for painting (see pages 6–8).

Use a variety of brushes for different effects. Sponge brushes are a good choice for larger spaces when applying acrylic and fabric paints or glue (if you are foiling). In fact, sponges of almost any description can be very effectively used for stenciling. Natural sponges make an interesting textured look. Synthetic household sponges are inexpensive, readily available, and come in a variety of textures. The larger the holes in the sponge, the rougher the texture of the finished results. If you have a fine-textured sponge and want a rougher look, gently pick small holes in the surface of your

Care and Cleaning of Embellished Surfaces

The gentlest, and to my mind best, way to clean embellished quilts is to vacuum them. There are a couple of methods you can use. The first is to put a nylon stocking over your vacuum's brush attachment and vacuum the quilt. As an alternative, you can also buy a piece of plastic window screening, place it over your quilt and vacuum through that.

Most paints, inks, and foils are washable. Check the manufacturer's instructions and follow them. My personal preference is to always err on the side of caution so, if laundering becomes an absolute necessity, I wash quilts in the bathtub using a mild soap and tepid water, rinsing well without ringing. For quilts or garments that need more frequent laundering, wash on the gentlest setting of your washing machine (turn garments inside out), using a mild soap and no bleach. Whichever method you use, dry both quilts and garments by either hanging or laying them flat.

Even when the manufacturer says it's okay, I avoid dry cleaning any painted or inked fabric because I don't trust commercial solutions to leave my work intact. Foil is never dry cleaned (or ironed, for that matter), because the adhesive will melt and the foil will come off.

As a general rule, if you treat your embellished quilts and quilted garments with respect, they will reward you with years of beauty and service.

sponge and make it into anything you want. Cosmetic sponges can be very handy because they are disposable and easy to cut into any shape. If you have a particularly tiny space you want to stencil, just dab your paint or glue on with a cotton swab.

When you are ready to stencil, cover your work surface with plastic to prevent making a mess. Lay the fabric out flat and either hold it in place with masking tape or iron it to freezer paper. Position the stencil and secure it in several places with masking tape. If there are parts of the stencil you don't want to use, use tape to mask them off. Pour some paint or glue onto a paper plate and dip your brush or sponge lightly in it. Remember, you can always add more but you can't take it away, so start with a fairly dry brush or sponge.

Using firm up-and-down motions, start at the outer edge and work your way toward the middle of the stencil. This technique helps prevent excess paint from seeping under the edges of the stencil and blurring the edges of your image. If you are going to paint on another color immediately, leave the stencil in place. Otherwise, when you are done, carefully lift the stencil straight up from the fabric so that you don't smudge. It's just that easy.

When you are finished, be sure to wash your brushes and sponges with a good brush cleaner or a conditioning shampoo and they will be in great shape for your next project. Wash any plastic stencil you have used, dry it well, and store it away from sunlight and dust. Remember, if you have been working with paint sticks, you will want to clean up everything you used with baby wipes or odorless mineral spirits.

IDEA GALLERY

EXPERIMENTATION is the spice of life! Take a look at these samples—what **EXCITES** your **IMAGINATION**? Gather together some basic materials and have a great time **PLAYING** with new **IDEAS** and techniques.

What to do when you've been asked to do a friendship block and have no time? Combining off-the-shelf stencils and paint sticks makes a unique and easy mock appliqué block. The assigned background fabric was a medium green, so I layered the paint to produce bolder colors.

Three stripes, three techniques, all painted on white fabric. On the left, wet fabric has been painted with runny paint. Because both paint and fabric are wet, the blue and yellow paints easily run together and make green. In the middle is an example of undiluted pink and red paints applied to dry fabric. On the right is the "sky" effect I wanted, which I achieved by using a foam brush to swish horizontal stripes of diluted blue paint onto wet fabric.

Fantasia, detail. Paint sticks made shading the leaves easy.

Fantasia, Melody Crust, 35" × 45." The flowers were appliqued and the leaves were all painted.

IDEA GALLERY

Sunscape, *Melody Crust, 4" × 6" Both positive and negative stencils can be used to great effect. The sun is a negative impression, using a regular plastic stencil. The positive star shapes were achieved by applying star stickers to the fabric, lightly dabbing paint around them, and peeling them off. (Any shape would work just as well.) The mountains were taped off with masking tape, and the foothills resulted from fancy paper cutting scissors applied to some scraps of freezer paper.*

View from the Top, *Melody Crust, 4" × 6." The same kinds of stencil materials were used here, but the finished product has a completely different look.*

Lavish Leaf, Melody Crust, 10" × 10." *My multi-talented friend, Heather Waldron, encourages me to make small samples of new ideas. This is a technique I experimented with and liked so much that I've used it in several different applications.*

IDEA GALLERY

*Pieced but unadorned background fabric used for **Daisy Delight**.*

Daisy Delight, *Melody Crust, 12" × 16." I used the same store-bought stencil here that I used in **Sweet Potato Vine** (see page 25). Here I arranged the painted leaves to form a perfect base for the embroidered daisies.*

Cape Cod Cherries, *Christine Palmer, quilted by Kate Sullivan, 60" × 70." Christine used an appliqué pattern but colored with crayons instead of traditional appliqué, producing this charming result.*

Painting white-on-white fabrics allows the underlying pattern to show through, creating a stunning new design.

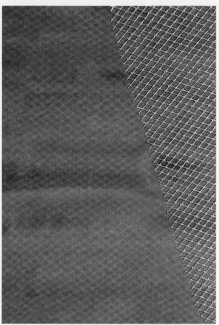

Try painting with Setacolor Transparent Paint (neatness does not count here) and placing a mesh fabric over the wet fabric. After sun drying, the result was the interesting texture on the left.

Drawing the flower outlines with a black paint pen and then immediately coloring them in with paint sticks made the colors merge slightly, producing a wonderful new color that added an extra dimension.

For a different, softer look, this paint stick-colored design was outlined using a matching-color paint pen.

BELOW RIGHT, **Garden Windows, Bendigo,** Carol Castaldi, 39" × 39". Inspired by a gated garden in Bendigo, Australia, this extravaganza of light and color is a dazzling work of art. TOP LEFT, **Garden Windows, Bendigo,** detail. Since her visit to Bendigo, Carol has refined her technique and cannot see fabric quilts as complete without beads, sequins, and other things. CENTER LEFT, **Garden Windows, Bendigo,** detail. Carol says, "Many people do not properly read a quilt like this—they see just a profusion of embellishments. There is not a single bead or sequin on any of my quilts that does not belong there." BOTTOM LEFT, **Garden Windows, Bendigo,** detail. What would a garden be without colorful flowers? These beauties have just been kissed by early morning dew.

2 BEADS, BUTTONS, AND MORE

It's a simple truth—**BEADS** are a blast! A quilt is a two-dimensional work of art. Add beads, buttons, or sew-on **JEWELS**, and you launch it straight into the realm of three-dimensional pizzazz. A sure-fire way to win admiration for a new garment is to add the **SPARKLE** and flair of sequins or shi-shas. Few of us can look at beading without a smile—beads and buttons just have that effect on people! Once you let beads **FIRE UP** your imagination, a whole world of possibilities opens up before you. Not only can you add **EMBELLISHMENTS** to the front of a quilt but to borders and even the label on the back as well. And just think what might happen if you turn your **CREATIVE** energies toward purses, vests, gloves, a child's sweater, or almost any type of **CLOTHING**, hand-made or off-the-rack. A quick stroll through the designer clothing section of any store (oh, those prices!) will tell you what **HIGH-END** manufacturers already know—adding beads, sequins, pearls, or rhinestones moves pretty much anything straight up the **STATUS** scale.

Eye Candy—bugle edge, Melody Crust, 2½" × 3½". Seed beads combined with bugle beads make a fast and colorful edge.

BEADS

There are any number of ways to use beads on your quilted projects. You can accent special stitches or highlight specific features, such as flowers, figures, baskets, or stars. A few single beads could add dew drops to a leaf, a string of them will quickly draw the eye to any particular part of a design that you want to emphasize. Imagine how delighted any little girl would be if you added a shiny bead fringe to her blouse, or how much a grown-up girl would love a sweater, jacket, or blouse that has been beautifully beaded.

Prep Work and Supplies

It's important to know that all beads are *not* created equal. Craft beads might cost less, but they are no bargain in the long run because they may tarnish, fade, or worse, run. Fashion beads, a much better choice, are generally washable and dry clean well. Clear and iridescent glass beads are usually colorfast, though some silver-lined glass beads may tarnish and turn black. White metal beads and charms can also discolor and stain your fabric. Before adding beads to your projects, take time to make sure that the beads you have chosen aren't going to disappoint you or ruin your work.

Variety of Beads

A basic bead is a round ball with one hole that goes straight through its center. Beads come in a wide variety of sizes, shapes, colors, finishes, and materials. They are typically sized and sold in millimeters, either in pre-packaged quantities, by the

This is just a small sample of the variety of beads available. There are large and small seed beads, bugles and twisted bugles, bone and hand-made beads, charms and trinkets, all just waiting for you to come play with them.

SUPPLIES CHECKLIST

✓ **BEADS** Use a variety of sizes, shapes, and materials. Have fun selecting them!

✓ **MASKING TAPE** Use to protect raw edges of fabric from fraying while beading. Blue painter's tape and paper medical tape also work well and leave no residue.

✓ **MARKERS** If you need to mark your fabric for bead placement, be sure to test first to ensure that the marks can be completely removed later.

✓ **SCISSORS**

Hand Beading Supplies

✓ **THREAD** Nymo thread, made of strong nylon, Silamide, and various silk threads are available in a range of colors and thicknesses. Use a single strand for sewing individual beads and a double strand for fringes and dangles. Do not use regular sewing thread, because glass bead edges will wear through it.

strand, by weight, or loose by the piece. Glass is the most common bead material. Glass beads can be transparent (light passes through completely), translucent (some light passes through), or opaque (no light passes through). *Iris* means that an iridescent coating has been applied, usually onto dark, opaque beads. *Matte* indicates an un-shiny finish. Glass beads can even be lined with colored metallics to give them a luster of gold, silver, or bronze.

Beads are also commonly made from bone, wood and even stone that is cut, polished, carved, and drilled into different shapes and sizes. Metal, brass, and aluminum can be stamped into uniquely shaped beads. Even plastic is a reliable and inexpensive alternative bead material. Visit any specialty bead store, and you will soon see that the choices are limitless, so let your imagination be your guide.

Use an embroidery hoop lined with felt to contain loose beads while you work. A 50¢ bead scoop makes capturing the beads and returning them to their container a snap.

Shopping for Beads

It's detrimental to the creative process to get too hung up in determining what you should buy—just get high quality beads you love, and you will find places to apply them! Most specialty bead shops, catalogs, or web sites organize beads according to color or according to the following general bead types.

- *Seed beads* are small, colorful beads, available either strung or loose. They are not particularly reflective of light, but add delightful dots of color and shine to garments or quilted projects. These are amazingly versatile beads—you are sure

✓ **QUILTING NEEDLES** I prefer to use number 10 large-eyed between (quilting) needles for beading because they allow me much better control than the longer needles designed for beading.

✓ **BEADING NEEDLES** Designed to help you pick up multiple beads at once, beading needles are long, thin, and very flexible, with a large eye. The higher the number, the thinner the needle. These are a challenge to control when attaching beads to fabric, so I tend to avoid them.

✓ **MILLINER NEEDLES** Use a number 9 Milliner for smaller beads and for fringes and dangles.

✓ **EMBROIDERY HOOP** If beading before quilting, use a 4″ × 9″ oval embroidery hoop to maintain tension. Wrap the inner hoop with twill tape to help grip the fabric without wrinkling it.

Machine Beading Supplies

✓ **FABRIC STABILIZER** Back quilt tops with a layer of batting before adding beads. Tear aways, spray starch, hoops, or water-soluble stabilizers are other viable options.

✓ **THREAD** If sewing by machine, use strong nylon or polyester bobbin thread both through the needle and in the bobbin. You may choose thread that matches or contrasts with the background fabric.

✓ **MACHINE NEEDLES** Sizes 80/12, 70/10, or, for really small beads, 60/8 are good choices. Needles used for machine beading should be small enough to go through the hole in the bead and small enough to slide easily between the beads. Begin with larger sizes before moving on to smaller needles.

✓ **TWEEZERS** Flat end tweezers are great for holding, controlling, and placing beads.

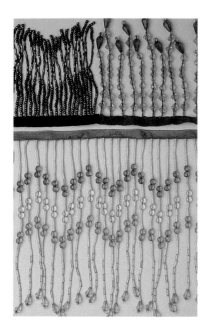

ABOVE LEFT, *A local sewing fair was the source of these wonderful beaded fringes. One has been used; the others are waiting for just the right spot to claim them.* ABOVE RIGHT, *Jewelry, old and new, an orphaned earring or two, a pendant without a chain—all are inexpensive sources of raw materials.*

to find a million and one uses for them. Seed beads are sized by number—the higher the number, the smaller the bead (size 11 is smaller than size 10). Widely available Czech beads are sold in hanks. They are commonly round but can sometimes be inconsistently sized. Japanese beads are more even in size. They come in a variety of colors and are usually sold loose. Delica brand seed beads are among my favorites—they are uniform in shape and size, and the relatively large hole at the center makes them a good choice for machine stitching.

- *Bugle beads* are tube-shaped and smooth on the outside. They are cut from small diameter glass tubes and come in multiple colors. About the width of a size 11 seed bead, they range in length from 2 mm to 40 mm (the larger the size number, the longer the bugle). Bugles are among the most reflective and sparkly of beads—wonderful for embellishing garments. Bugles are often sold along with seed beads, and the pairing is known as *treasure beads*.

- *Faceted beads* are made to shine. They are available in a huge array of colors and sizes, in inexpensive plastic and wonderful glass.

- *Drops* are, as their name implies, beads that are beautifully shaped in the form of teardrops. The hole is at the top, at the narrow pointed end. Drops are perfect for making beaded fringes that dangle from a garment or purse.

- *Beaded fringe* is great for jumpstarting a new project. Ready made, the fringe is already beaded. There are a zillion types and colors available—and someone else did all the work!

As well as these bead types, shops and catalogs often offer *fancy* beads—which quite simply means anything with a hole in it that you can sew through!

And, remember, don't limit yourself to bead shops or craft stores—when it comes to collecting beads, the whole world is your mega-mart. Treasures can be found by rummaging through your jewelry box or wardrobe. Scan yard and estate sales for loose beads, jewelry, or clothing missing a bead or two. Often you can find handcrafted, one-of-a-kind beads at street fairs and festivals. A friend's recent visit to a thrift store yielded a dress that was completely covered with the most beautiful glass

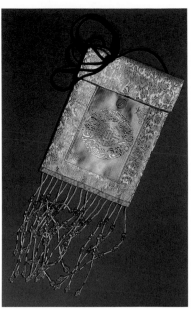

beads—and priced at one dollar! Check online, too—search words such as *bead*, *rhinestone*, or *sequin*, and you will be deluged with choices.

Pre-Testing Beads

Look carefully at beads before you buy them. If you notice blobs of color, especially around holes, the color is probably not permanent. To test beads for colorfastness,

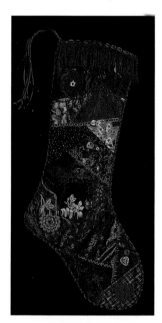

Christmas Stocking, Melody Crust. Just because a bead, trim, or trinket turns out to not be completely colorfast doesn't mean I don't still love it. What better place to use these goodies than a Christmas stocking that will never be laundered?

wash them vigorously in water mixed with a few drops of bleach. Rinse well, then dry in a paper towel. If there are small flakes of paint in the towel, the beads are not colorfast. To check for fading, compare washed beads against unwashed beads. If the washed beads are noticeably lighter in color, they will definitely fade, probably with no more provocation than the exposure to light and sun that happens with just the passage of time.

Another testing method is to sew a few beads onto a scrap of fabric and launder it at the same water temperature and with the same soap you would use on a finished project. If you plan on dry cleaning, take your test swatch to the cleaners before making the garment. Check the beads carefully after cleaning to see if you are satisfied with the results.

Care and Storage

Be kind to your beads by storing them in a cool, dry location and avoiding extremes of heat, humidity, and dampness. Store your beads in clear film canisters, zip-lock bags, or other recycled containers. To be very organized, glue a bead to the outside of each container so that you can find what you need at a glance.

ABOVE LEFT, **Beaded Bracelets,** Melody Crust and Heather Waldron. I love all things beaded; these bracelets are not only fun to wear, they inspire me to hurry up and start working on my next embellishment project. ABOVE RIGHT, *Fringed green bag. If you want a fast way to jazz up an old favorite or need a gift at a moment's notice, this is the way to go. A purchased bag, a few inches of luxurious beaded fringe, and ten minutes later, you're all set.*

Take special care when ironing beaded garments. Glass beads can get hot enough to harm the surrounding fabric or thread with which they are attached. If a beaded item needs to be pressed, either steam it without touching the fabric or the beads, or use a thick pressing cloth. Alternatively, place your project face down onto a fluffy towel and then press it from the back.

Bead Placement

One of the joys of embellishing with beads is that there is no real need to plan your designs ahead of time. You can start by choosing beads of a particular type or color, or even with a random sample of mixed beads, then design as-you-go! You can make beading decisions one at a time as your work develops. Often, there is no need to mark your fabrics. Look for patterns in the fabric or appliqués or look for other built-in guides like polka dots to help you decide the right bead placement. Plaids or checks absolutely invite you to sew beads either at the intersections or in the centers of the pattern. Beads placed in the centers of flowers add a wonderful sparkle and

RIGHT, *Mardi Gras*, Melody Crust, *28″ × 28″. I add beads and other embellishments after I quilt because it is easier for me to make design decisions when I can see the whole picture—fabrics, quilting, and beads—all together.* ABOVE, *Mardi Gras, detail. This quilt traveled with a national show for over a year. I was certain that when it finally came home, beads would be missing. Fortunately, I had sewn through all the larger beads three or four times. There were a couple of broken threads, but all the beads were still there and mending it was easy.*

LEFT, ***Spotlight***, *Melody Crust,
19" × 19". I explored this traditional
orange peel pattern in a new way,
employing beads, buttons, ribbon,
and fancy fabrics.* ABOVE, ***Spotlight***,
*detail. Your fabrics will often tell you
where to place the beads, so be sure
to look closely.*

depth. You can add beads to highlight a particular detail or colors and, of course, motifs are easy to embellish—any *Sun Bonnet Sue*, for instance, would be proud to wear a string-of-beads hat band. And remember, you can also place beads on lace, ribbons, buttons, or silk ribbon embroidery, or with just about any combination of techniques or materials you devise. The possibilities are infinite!

If you decide to mark a particular design before you begin beading, use a quality quilting marker that will disappear from your work without leaving any unwelcome residue. If in doubt, test your marking tool to ensure that the marks can be completely removed later.

Beading by Hand

Hand-sewing works very well after a piece is quilted. Easy, fast, and satisfying, it gives you absolute control over where each bead is positioned. My best advice is to approach the task exactly as you would hand quilting. Thread a needle with a single strand of Nymo thread, about 25" long, and place a quilter's knot at the end. Start about ½" away from the first bead location and "pop" the knot between the layers of the quilt or quilted garment. Come up at the point where the first bead will be placed. Put the point of the needle into the bead and push it onto the needle with the tip of your finger. The stitch you make needs to be just as long as the diameter

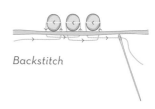

Backstitch

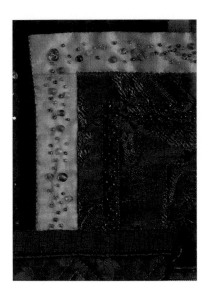

RIGHT, **1936**, Melody Crust, 15″ × 17″. Breathing new life into some of the best of the old styles with modern techniques and fabrics can be a challenge. Here, beads highlight the geometry of a wonderful art deco design. ABOVE LEFT, **1936**, detail. The act of hand sewing lots of beads is very soothing, so I enjoyed the process of scattering different beads in order to help the design get the attention I thought it deserved.

of the bead—any longer and the thread will show; any shorter, the bead won't lie flat. Take a second stitch through every third or fourth bead—if the thread should ever break, two or three beads will come off, but not the whole group. As an extra precaution, run the thread through bigger, heavier beads three or four times. Keep going until you come to the end of your thread and finish as you would for a line of hand quilting.

There are several stitching techniques you can use to sew beads to fabric. Here are some of my favorites.

Basic Bead Stitch

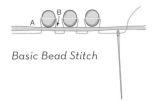

Basic Bead Stitch

This most basic beading stitch is fast, fun, and simple to accomplish. Use a running stitch to apply duplicate beads in straight, even rows. Come up at point A, right next to where you want to place the bead, pop the bead onto your needle and go back down into the fabric at B, just at the end of the bead.

Scattering Beads

Use a basic bead stitch, but this time vary the distance between the beads for a scattered effect. This random placement of either the same or a variety of beads adds extra interest.

Bugle Stacking

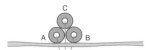

Bugle stacking is a slight variation of the basic bead stitch, creating a beautiful bump of texture of bugle beads on your fabric. Stitch through bead A, then place bead B next to it and stitch. Stack bead C on top of A and B and sew through it, too.

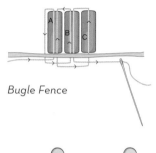

Bugle Stacking

Bugle Fence

Putting short bugle beads on end makes them stand up and be noticed. Sew up through bead A, then down the outside of bead A (to the left for right-handed stitchers). Position bead B next to bead A, then stitch up through bead B and down through bead A. Continue to the end of your fence.

Bugle Fence

Grouped Seeds

This is another backstitch variation, this time with seed beads. Group an uneven number of beads together in any combination of colors you wish. Bring your needle up at point A, string it though a group of beads, and bring it down at B. The space between A and B depends on the number and size of the beads and the size of the raised bump you desire.

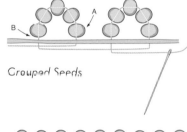

Grouped Seeds

Scattering Beads

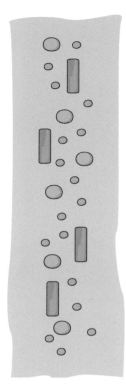

Beading in Straight and Curved Lines

Long, straight rows of beads can be a challenge to sew—a little practice goes a long way! Use the basic stitch (single strand of thread) until the line of beads is the length you want. Bead a curved line by stitching around a curve. Always make corrections to accommodate the curve when your needle comes up. To strengthen and straighten your lines of beading, bring a new thread on a long Milliner needle up from the back side of your project, just underneath the last stitch. Enter the "tunnel" of beads and exit when it becomes difficult to travel further. *Don't* stitch back into the fabric yet, but continue on through the tunnel. Keep going like this until you reach the end of the line. Give your thread a slight tug and the beads will adjust themselves perfectly. Knot your thread and you are done!

Straight Lines

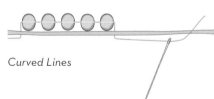

Curved Lines

Couching

A simple technique known as *couching* can be done with either one thread or two. The two-thread method is a bit easier to do; the one thread method allows you to make spontaneous decisions on which bead you want to add next.

For the two-thread method, either string or restring the beads onto a very strong thread, such as Nymo. (If you don't, sooner or later, the thread will snap and you

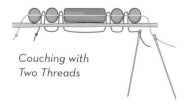

Couching with Two Threads

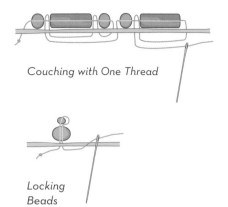

Couching with One Thread

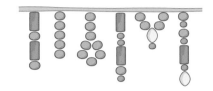

Locking Beads

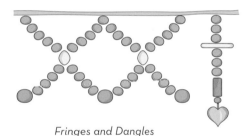

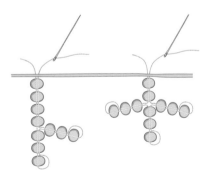

Fringes and Dangles

will lose beads.) Lay the beaded strand directly onto the fabric and secure the end of the thread with a pin. Use a second Nymo thread to stitch over (couch) the first thread every three or four beads. For smooth curves, you will need to make more frequent stitches. Remove the pin, bring both threads to the back and secure them.

You can also couch using a single thread by backstitching as shown. Using a double thickness of Nymo thread, make and hide a knot. Pull the thread to where the first bead will be placed and string six to eight beads on your needle. At the end of the beaded group, push the needle back into the fabric and come up back three or four beads. Stitch up and over the thread. To get your needle back in position to sew more beads, push it under the fabric again, come up, and continue stitching.

Locking Beads

Securely attach large beads, sequins, charms, trinkets, or buttons using a locking bead. Begin by popping the knot, then string one large bead (or whatever) onto your thread. Follow the large bead with a smaller one, remembering that the small bead has to be bigger than the hole of the large bead. Pass the needle back through the hole of the large bead, going around the outside of the smaller bead. Pull the thread completely through to the wrong side of the fabric and secure it.

Bead Fringes and Dangles

Fringes are composed of a series of bead strands that create a decorative border. *Dangles* are just a single fringe. The variations are endless, and each one you see is more tempting than the last.

To begin a fringe, double your thread. Pull the needle and thread through the fabric and pop the knot. Add a series of beads to make up your first strand, then add a locking bead. Take your needle back through all of the beads, except for the locking bead. Continue until your fringe is the length you want, then pull the thread all the way through to the back side of your fabric and knot it securely.

Full Fringe

A very effective variation of fringe, this lets you include lots more beads, too! Make a small stitch and string beads onto the thread to the desired length. Pass the needle around the outside of the locking bead and push it back through part of the beads on the string. Add more beads to your thread, again skip the locking bead, and pass your needle through the rest of the beads on your original string. Make a stitch and continue.

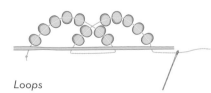

Full Fringe

Loops

An informal looping of beads, either on the edges or in the body of a quilt or garment, makes a graceful pattern. The threading is simple—just make sure you use a strong thread. To loop, make a stitch, then slide the beads onto some doubled Nymo thread. Put your needle back into the fabric at the end of the desired loop and out again about halfway into your last loop. Add more beads and continue on.

Loops

Picots

Picot beading is fast, easy, and trouble free—not to mention charming. Just thread and sew as shown, working this pretty pattern along a border or decorative edge. Three beads on your thread and a backstitch only one bead wide forces the beads to "picot."

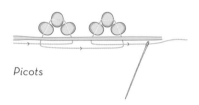

Picots

Scalloped Edge

This soft edging, done in colorful seed beads, is dynamite! Fast and easy, it secures beads prettily along any edge. Take a small stitch in your work, slide seven beads onto the thread. Make another small stitch, then return your needle through the first two beads. Slide five beads onto your thread and make a small stitch. Continue sewing, adding five beads at a time. If you go around corners, you will need to add an extra bead or two in order to keep your beading flat.

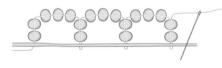

Scalloped Edge

Beading Buttons

Use a covered button blank that can be found at any fabric store. Cover it with your chosen fabric in the way the package directs you. Pop your initial knot, sew on your beads, buttons, sequins, etc., and finish up by popping the last knot.

Beading by Machine

When machine embellishing, I find that adding the beads *after* sandwiching and machine quilting is the easier way to go. If you are beading a hand-made garment, you have the option to bead before the final assembly. Obviously, if the item is off-the-rack, you will be beading directly onto the finished piece.

Beads can be sewn onto some amazing places, including these covered buttons.

Eye Candy with Yellow Picot Edge,
Melody Crust, 2½" × 3½". A simple
yellow picot edge repeats the yellow
of the flowers, which helps balance
the design.

Machine Couching

Free Motion Couching

There are two approaches to beading by machine. *Couching* is fast and easy. Sewing one bead at a time—*free motion*—is more challenging but certainly an option for those who prefer to use their machine for everything. With both methods, it is important to secure the threads at the points where you start and stop. If you are working with a single layer of fabric, bring both threads to the top of the work, then make 10 to 15 very small stitches in the first quarter inch. Clip the tails close to the fabric. To finish a row of stitching, make the same tiny stitches and, again, clip the threads. If you are working with layers, pull all tails to the back and tie surgeon's knots. Next, thread the ends through a large-eyed hand-sewing needle and bury them between the layers, clipping any loose ends. I prefer to do it this way whenever possible because I think it looks neater.

Machine Couching

Couching is the easiest way to stitch beads by machine. It is done using a cording, piping, or beading foot that will accommodate the beads. With the feed dogs up, use a zig zag or a blind hem stitch. Place the appropriate foot on your machine and thread the string of beads through the hole in the foot. Make a test sample to determine the best stitch length, then sew.

Begin by stringing loose beads or transferring beads that are already on a hank onto Nymo thread using a hand-sewing needle. The thread your beads came on is very weak and not trustworthy for couching. Tie a small knot and slide your beads off of the original (weak) string and onto a length of Nymo thread. *Do not* cut the thread from the Nymo spool yet, because the beads are going to want to shift just a bit as you sew, and this gives them some room to do so. It also means your beads can't get loose and end up all over the floor. Set your machine to zigzag and carefully stitch over the string of beads. As an extra precaution, I usually fasten off both ends of the thread the beads are on by threading them through a hand-sewing needle and securing them on the back of my work.

Free Motion Couching

Lowering the feed dogs allows you to stitch in any direction. I prefer to use an open-toe free-motion foot, but another option would be to not use a foot at all. If you choose to sew without a foot, a hoop is an absolute necessity for stability. Stitch small securing stitches, then free motion sew over your bead-laden Nymo thread. End with more securing stitches. Another tip—this is the time to use a straight stitch throat plate (with a small round hole instead of the standard oval), if you have one.

Free Motion Beading

Adding one bead at a time by machine takes some practice, but can be accomplished. It is very liberating to be able to drop the feed dogs and sew in any direction you please. If you are reasonably proficient at free-motion machine quilting, do try this technique. The object is to turn the pretty side of the bead up. This technique works best with seed beads of 6 mm or smaller that have a hole large enough to accommodate the machine needle. Sequins and charms can also be attached in this way.

Set your machine for free motion stitching (lower the feed dogs). Some sort of stabilizer is necessary. It can be a sandwiched quilt, a hoop, or any stabilizer you prefer. Try a couple of methods to see what works best for you. Stitch up to where you want to place your bead. When you are ready to begin, slide the first bead onto the needle (tweezers make this job easier). Make your first stitch at point A. The next stitch should be placed tight next to the bead, but on the other side of it, at B. The third stitch goes on top of the first stitch, at point C. Place the fourth stitch on top of the second, at point D. Free motion stitch to the next bead.

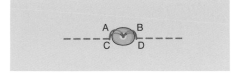

Free Motion Beading by Machine

Neptune's Weave, *Melody Crust, 43″ × 54″. One of my first forays into beading by machine, this project taught me that machine couching beads is fun, but I prefer the tactile pleasure of applying the individual beads by hand.*

ABOVE LEFT, **Spotlight,** *detail. The button placement and black stitching serve to highlight the flowers in the gold fabric. See full quilt on page 43.* RIGHT, *Pearls, sequins, hot-fix and glue-on beads and sparkles.*

BEYOND BEADS: PEARLS, SEQUINGS, JEWELS, AND SHI-SHAS

What fun it is to live in this glorious age of embellishment! As much as I love beads, other "fancies" are every bit as much fun. Explore quilt, bead and craft stores, thrift shops, catalogs, and the internet for sequins, pearls, jewels, shi shas, and crystals. Everywhere you look there are tempting beauties; elegant, colorful, witty and spectacular, ready and willing to take your work to the next level. So use whatever strikes your fancy and don't limit yourself to just beads.

Prep Work and Supplies

A wide variety of beautiful non-bead embellishments is available from quilt or craft stores, either pre-packaged or loose. Most are ready to sew or attach to your projects and need no advance preparation. If you plan on washing the quilt or garment after you embellish it, make a test swatch of fabric and affix some sample sequins, jewels, or pearls to it. Wash it as you plan to wash the finished work before committing to your selection of embellishments.

Pearls

Pearls never fail to add a touch of elegance and, of course, are always popular for heirloom projects such as wedding dresses, christening outfits, and associated accessories. From freshwater pearls to cultured pearls to uniquely shaped baroque pearls and multi-sized craft pearls, there is a choice for

SUPPLIES CHECKLIST

You will need few other sewing supplies than those needed for beading, see pages 38 to 39. Also keep close to hand some two-sided tape and some glue.

Duchess, *Melody Crust, 2½″ × 3½″. The pearls lend just a touch of class to this soft, delicate work.*

LEFT, **Plum Blossom**, Melody Crust, 27" × 32". Oriental designs fascinate me. The sequins of the floral appliqué accent are meant to add dimension, and the layered fans and lamé fabrics provide movement. ABOVE RIGHT, **Plum Blossom**, detail. An unexpected element, such as these sequins, can add interest to a quilt.

every project and every budget. White is not the only color option—you can find pearls in several pastel shades, including blue, gray, pink, ivory, champagne, green, and lavender. You may even come across black pearls when you need them. The shape, too, varies and while perfectly round pearls are typical, a little searching will yield other varieties, such as teardrop pearls or oat pearls (also known as rice beads or wheat beads). Most often, pearls are sold pre-strung or pre-packaged with holes drilled through the center, making them as easy to work with as beads—but how lovely they are!

Affix pearls just as you would beads (see pages 44 to 45). I prefer to use silk thread on heirloom projects, such as wedding dresses, but Nymo is a good choice when sturdiness and longevity are important. Most made-for-clothing pearls can be laundered and dry cleaned, but to be sure about the pearls you purchase, always test them first. Be aware, for instance, that craft pearls are not washable and will lose their pearl finish if ironed.

Sequins

Sequins come in more shapes, finishes, sizes, and colors than I can possibly list. Flat, cupped, or square, transparent, iridescent, or opaque, and available in any color of the rainbow, their variety is glorious. You can find sequins anywhere, either loose or on strings, and they are generally sized from 3 mm to 50 mm.

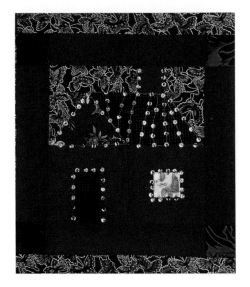

LEFT, *Machine stitched "lights" playfully decorate this house for Christmas.* RIGHT, *Don't forget the tree outside!*

Because the finishes and quality of sequins vary so greatly there is no single answer as to how best to care for them. Some can't be laundered and others won't tolerate dry cleaning. Testing your sequins, just like you would test beads, is the only way to decide if your finished project can be safely washed (see page 41).

Attaching by Hand

A beautiful way to attach sequins is to pair them with small beads, using a bead to lock each sequin in place. Simply bring your needle up through the fabric then through the sequin and bead. Bring it around the bead, then back through the sequin

Straight off-the-rack, a basically un-adorned woman's shirt seems a bit blah. . . . Just top-stitch the ribbon, add beads and colorful thread—this shirt is now ready to party! If you think to sew the fringe to loop tape and sew its companion side to your garment (oops, I didn't!), it will be very easy to remove the fringe prior to washing. The cufflinks were handmade with just buttons and beads.

Embellishing Garments

Beading and embellishing have the power to transform the ordinary into the extraordinary. When considering which garments are worthy of your beading artistry, look for details such as front bands, collars, cuffs, pockets, yokes, and hems—these are perfect for embellishing with beads (and for some creative top-stitching, too). If the garment has buttons down the front, that opens up a whole new set of possibilities. Not only can you replace plain buttons with wonderful, unique ones, you can also bead around the existing buttons, or even sew beads onto the button tops. Make sure that any decoration that is already part of the selected garment will not fight with your fancy work. Solid color fabrics usually show off embellishments best, but you can also successfully add beads, jewels, or pearls to stripes, as long as they aren't too busy. If you are buying a garment off-the-rack with the intention of embellishing it, stick with items that can be laundered by hand and fabrics that need little or no ironing. Remember the weight of a selected and into the fabric. I recommend using Nymo thread, though a strong polyester thread will also hold them firmly in place. Of course, you can also sew on sequins without the beads by bringing the thread up through the sequin and then down over the edge as many times as you need to suit your design or secure the sequin in place. For added effect, try using a contrasting thread and showing off your stitching as well as your sequins!

Attaching by Machine

Sequins can easily be stitched over—or *couched*—by machine using an embroidery foot. An open-toed embroidery foot, which allows you to see what is happening, makes this even easier. The trick to sewing strings of sequins is to be aware of their direction. Run your fingers along the string and notice that they feel like fish scales. Be sure to sew with the flow of the scales, not against it.

Sew-on Jewels

Craft jewels typically have flat backs and a mirror finish, making them simple to sew and giving them lots of sparkle. You can sew them in place as easily as beads, using the holes that are pre-drilled through them.

Round sew-on rhinestones are usually secured by a metal bracket on the back, with two or more holes through which to pass your thread. Rhinestones are also available by the yard, pre-attached to a special webbing. This makes them remarkably quick and easy to sew onto your project. One precaution—make sure the metal bracket is stainless steel to avoid potential problems with rusting.

embellishment may affect the drape of your garment. Knits or any stretchy fabric will require a lightweight cut-away stabilizer. Putting the area of fabric you are working on in a hoop makes stitching much easier.

Once you have selected a garment, plan your design. Choose a single type of embellishment, such as beads or sequins, or try mixing different types together. Arrange them on the fabric in either parallel or staggered rows. Vary the sizes and colors. Decide whether you want to group beads or other embellishments together or if you would prefer to scatter them. Is there a particular design that would really enhance a particular garment? Or is there a special theme or motif that will especially please the wearer? So many choices, so many beads and baubles! What could be more fun?

It's easier to machine top stitch a garment before you bead rather than after. Take a few moments to consider the weight and number of thicknesses of the fabric. A single thickness of a very lightweight fabric will definitely need some sort of stabilizer, perhaps just a double thickness of the same fabric or some interfacing. A heavier fabric or a part of the garment that has several layers of fabric (such as a collar) probably won't need any extra stabilizer at all.

Consider using a single colored thread, a variegated thread, or two or more different colors combined to achieve different looks. Try two threads through the needle at one time. Or use several colors of beads and a different thread to match each one. If you particularly want to show off the thread, set your machine for a slightly longer stitch. For a finish that is both pretty and professional looking, leave the thread tails three or four inches long at the end of each of your rows. Pull the ends to the wrong side of your garment, knot them and bury the ends. Remember that if you want to surround your embellishments with thread, you will need one more row of stitching than rows of beading in order to form an outline.

Reflections, Melody Crust, 2½" × 3½". *These mirrored flower centers are held in place with hand-dyed perle cotton thread.*

Generally speaking, sew-on jewels and rhinestones can be machine washed and air dried, but not dry cleaned. If in doubt, test a sample before sewing them onto your quilts or garments.

Shi-Sha Mirrors

Traditional shi-sha mirrors are made from mica flakes, but real mirrors are now more readily available and are much more durable. Shi-shas are usually round, though you can also find triangles, squares, and other shapes. Most shi-sha mirrors can be successfully washed or dry cleaned, but check the manufacturer's directions or test them yourself as you would test beads.

Attaching by Hand

The embroidery around a shi-sha is usually a very close buttonhole stitch done with perle cotton, crochet thread, or silk ribbon. Embroidery floss can be used with three or six or even twelve strands for a heavy-threaded look. You might want to add some metallic threads through the same needle for extra glitter.

It's easy to attach shi-sha mirrors by hand. Start by sewing a tic-tac-toe grid of stitches across the mirror. Then embroider by bringing your needle up through the fabric at the edge of the shi-sha, looping it through the center grid, gently pulling the center square of your

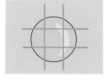

Shi-Shas by Hand

tic-tac-toe design back just a bit to form a frame around the glass and pushing your needle back into the fabric. Continue all the way around.

Attaching by Machine

Attach shi-shas by machine by stitching a small, round buttonhole slightly smaller than your shi-sha and cutting it out. Turn your work over and lay the mirror, face down, over the hole. If you have two-sided tape on hand, it can make holding everything in place much easier. Position another small piece of fabric over the mirror, leaving just enough edge to allow you to either glue or stitch around it. Attach the fabric by either method and you are done!

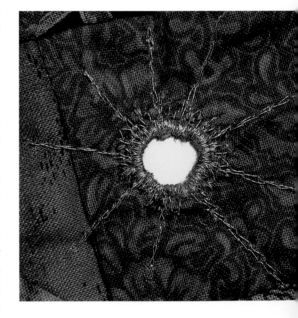

A machine applied shi-sha mirror.

Moonbeam, Melody Crust, 3½" × 2½". Hot-fix crystals add instant glitz.

HOT-FIX CRYSTALS

Practical and easy to apply, hot-fix crystals can jazz up anything in minutes! These little beauties are heat resistant, sparkling crystals that have a special glue already applied to the backs which, when melted, permanently attaches them to fabric. They can be purchased loose or as appliqués temporarily attached to a backing in a decorative pattern.

Crystal Appliqués

Crystal appliqués, whether for monograms, motifs, or intricate designs, come in all shapes and sizes and are available at quilt shops, craft stores, or specialty catalogs and web sites. To affix crystal appliqués to your project, begin by removing any backing and cutting off any excess clear plastic. This allows for more precise placement of the appliqué. Make sure that every one of the crystals is properly placed before you begin. Misplaced stones can be repositioned as you work with a pair of tweezers. Working on a hard, flat surface, position the appliqué onto the fabric and cover with a press cloth. Using a dry iron on the "wool" setting and with medium pressure, put the iron straight down on top of the design, being careful not to move it around. Press for about 30 seconds—a bit longer for heavy fabrics and less for light ones. Allow the appliqué to cool completely, then remove the remaining plastic. After ironing, the crystals are permanently attached.

Once applied, some crystals can be gently machine washed and dried or dry cleaned (check the manufacturer's instructions). *Never* use chlorine bleach. If you need to iron your project, press the wrong side with a dry iron or use a press cloth.

Wild About Flowers, *Melody Crust. Okay, so once in a while my trusty hot glue gun gets called into action. This hat, made for a charity auction, just needed an extra something to put it right over the top, so I glued on clear jewels as dewdrops.*

Attaching Single Crystals Using a Hot-Fix Tool

Single hot-fix crystals are available loose in an endless array of colors, sizes, and shapes, which allows you the option of creating your own design. Each one comes backed with a unique glue which, when melted with a special hot-fix tool, permanently attaches it to fabric. This tool gets extremely hot, so be sure to follow the manufacturer's safety instructions.

Most hot-fix tools come with a variety of different sized tips. Always choose the tip size that best fits the crystal you are applying. It's easy to use the applicator tip to pick up the crystals—practice on a sample swatch of fabric with a few loose crystals until you get the hang of it. Since the tool gets hot, wear gloves or be careful to not let it touch your skin.

Use the tip to pick up a crystal, wait a few seconds until the adhesive on the back begins to look shiny and melted, then apply it straight down onto the fabric and lift the tool back up, releasing the crystal. Carefully check to make sure the crystal adhered properly.

If you have difficulty picking up crystals with the hot-fix tool, use a pair of tweezers in your dominant hand. Pick up a crystal (glue side down), position it, and hold it in place. With your other hand, position the hot-fix tool on top of the crystal and remove the tweezers. Hold both tool and crystal in place for approximately 25 seconds, then let the crystal cool. If you'd like to take an extra precaution, use a toothpick to hold the crystal in place when you remove the tool to help keep your fingers out of harm's way.

Hot-fixed crystals can usually be machine washed and air dried or dry cleaned; just be sure to either pre-test or read the manufacturer's instructions to be safe.

BUTTONS

Buttons are such a part of our everyday world that we sometimes neglect to see how fun and decorative they can be. After all, what is a button but a somewhat flattened bead that moonlights as a closure? Buttons offer a quick and easy way to enhance embroidery, fashion design, and decorative quilting. Whether they are made from precious metals, bone, porcelain, or workaday plastic, buttons come in a virtually limitless array of shapes and sizes—the choice is all yours!

Prep Work and Supplies

Buttons require no special attention or treatment before sewing onto your projects. As with other embellishments, take time to test that they are washable before committing to them. Some buttons can't be laundered; others won't stand up to dry cleaning. The same testing methods for beads should be done with buttons. If you find an irresistible button that absolutely cannot be washed, check your craft store for special safety pins that let you attach and remove buttons as desired. It's a snap to take them off before laundering—the only hard part is remembering to do it.

If you keep an eye out for them, buttons are waiting to be discovered in all kinds of places. When was the last time you really sifted through your grandmother's button box or, for that matter, rummaged through your own? Everything old is new again, as the saying goes, and who knows what unusual or vintage treasures may be sitting there, waiting for you to rescue them? Your local thrift shop is a terrific place to purchase loose buttons and, while you are there, be sure to glance through the used clothing for interesting and inexpensive buttons.

Selecting Buttons

As you begin a new project, take a moment to contemplate how the humble button may affect your design. You can use buttons to enhance the overall feel you want to achieve on a newly designed garment. Select small, delicate buttons for a feminine touch; clean, timeless styles for classic designs; or whimsical novelty buttons for a fun, fashion look that is exactly on theme. Jeweled or pearl buttons are very elegant, and rhinestone buttons are definitely on the extravagant side.

Buttons give us all a wonderful opportunity to think outside of the box. If you don't have the exact size and number of buttons a clothing pattern calls for, think of this as a blessing in disguise. You might end up with a much more interesting and unusual look by adjusting your spacing to accommodate an alternate button size or by using fewer or more buttons than intended. Contrary to popular opinion, the buttons don't have to match exactly as long as there is some unifying element: color, size, texture, style, or material. Be sure to check both sides of your buttons—the backs are often as interesting as the fronts! One more tip—dress up almost any button by sewing it on with a contrasting colored thread.

Creative Button Embellishments

When it comes to dreaming up new ways to use buttons, the sky is the limit. I enjoy using them to emphasize particular parts of a design, whether I am working on a quilt top, a garment, or fashion accessories. By stacking different-sized buttons, you can give extra dimension to a particular motif, such as the center of a star patch or the flap on a purse. Try using a tiny, delicate button at the center of an embroidered flower. Sew a piece of

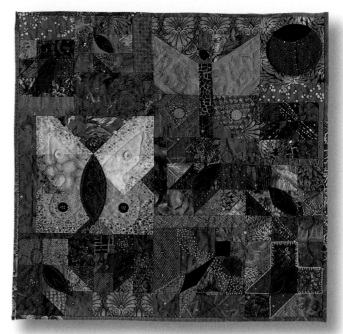

Heebee Jeebee, Melody Crust, 20″ × 24″. Inspired by millions of Monarch butterflies wintering in Angangueo, Mexico, this quilt just had to be colorful.

Heebee Jeebee, detail. Butterflies are adorned with all kinds of dots and spots, so my button and bead collections saw some heavy use.

This assortment of buttons includes some really large ones that my friends said are just too big to use, but it turns out they work very well as purse closures. Tiny buttons always make wonderful flower centers and accents. The hand-painted and theme buttons are still waiting for a home.

fancy trim on top of a particularly large button, or use a piece of narrow ribbon, yarn or thread to tie the button to your fabric.

I also like to blend buttons with other embellishments. Beads, for instance, are perfect for locking buttons in place. In fact, a four-hole button just cries out for four or more beads to be sewn on top of it. A button at the base of a dangle adds a special flair to any string of beads. Combine your buttons with sequins or glue-on crystals, or sew on single pearls for special effects that will delight you each time you look at them.

Covered buttons are a unique way to take your project to the next level. Add extra beauty with a minimum of effort or expense by covering buttons with tiny scraps of vintage fabric. Try covering several buttons with fabric from different areas of an embroidered hand towel. For an entirely different look, cover oversize buttons with pieces cut from a colorful tablecloth. Take a piece of fabric you have stenciled or stamped with paint or ink and use it to cover a button—and remember that you can always add embroidery or beads to the top!

If you still can't find that perfect button for the effect you desire, modify! Take a Sharpie or other favorite marker and draw the pattern or motif

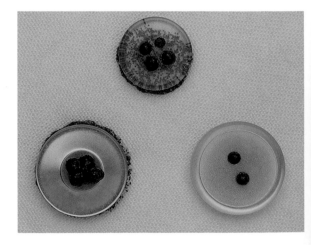

Finish your project quickly by using paint to secure the button as well as to decorate it.

As an experiment, I decided to ink some buttons with permanent markers. I was having so much fun—I just couldn't stop!

you're looking for directly onto the button. To increase its durability, spray the button afterwards with a fixative.

Decorating Button Holes

Not only can you decorate buttons, you can dress up the buttonholes, too! Once you've chosen your buttons and figured out where they are going to be positioned, take a few moments to look closely at that portion of your design. Before making the button hole, consider jazzing up that space by appliquéing vintage, painted, embroidered, or other special fabric over it.

Fancy stitching is another lovely option when decorating a buttonhole. Hand-stitch with embroidery floss, or with cotton or silk buttonhole twist thread that matches the rest of the design. Mark the placement line on the right side of your fabric and machine-stitch a rectangle around it, ⅛″ from your placement line. Cut along the line and finish by hand, using small blanket stitches. Fan out the stitches along each end to accommodate the rectangular shape. For added strength, bar-tack across the ends of your rectangle.

Once the button is in place, that is no reason to stop. Take one last look and you may have more embellishment ideas. A star-shaped appliqué framing that pretty star button on the cuff might look very cute. Make sure your cutout is slightly larger than the button so that it shows up well. (You might want to start with a shape larger than you think you need and trim as necessary.) A circle appliqué—or even a tiny ring of embroidered roses—might set off a plain round button to perfection. My message here is, once you think you are finished—look again. One more embellishment might be all your garment needs!

IDEA GALLERY

So many beads, **BAUBLES**, and trinkets . . . so little time! Look through these **SAMPLES** for some **POSSIBLE** places to start, then thread your needle and come out **SEWING!**

Mirabella, unembellished.

Mirabella, Melody Crust, 2½″ × 3½″. Bedazzled with lots of sequins.

The impact of this quilted heart changes dramatically with the addition of beads.

Love Potion, *label. I "skootch" the ribbon with the point of my needle, then sew on a bead to hold it in place. See full quilt on page 62.*

Love Potion*, Melody Crust, 10" × 12". Floppy ribbons
didn't look right, so I buttoned them down.*

As you can see, there is quite a difference between the painted button and the untouched original sitting to one side. The foliage is inked, the flower petals are done in appliqué.

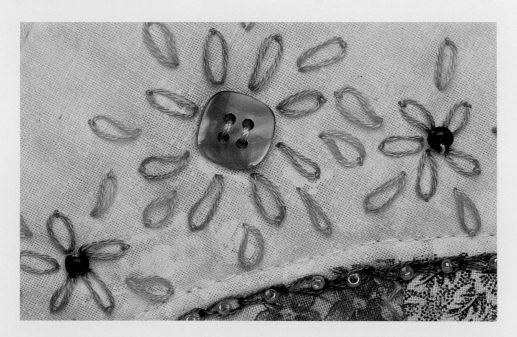

Buttons make perfect centers for embroidered flowers.

Eye Candy with Six Point Fringe, Melody Crust, 2½″ × 3½″. A pieced background and painted leaves with the edges quilted using shiny thread still needed a bit of "pop," so it got a beaded fringe, too.

This off-the-shelf bag was beautifully embroidered but needed some sparkle, so I beaded it, being careful to enhance, not obscure, the embroidery.

An inexpensive gift bag looks like a million with the addition of a fancy cord and a fast bead fringe.

All Dressed for School, Melody Crust, 30" × 20". When your darling sister loves the idea of an aquarium but hates the fuss, and Christmas is fast approaching . . . .

All Dressed for School, detail. Beads personalize a preprinted fish.

Eye Candy with Yellow Full Fringe, Melody Crust, 3½" × 2½". Sometimes, it's hard to tell how much is enough. When in doubt, add more!

Eye Candy with Buttons, Melody Crust, 2½" × 3½". The buttons and beads are the intended focus of this piece. Even though it's fused, the pesky border tried to ravel, so I blanket stitched it with variegated thread and loved how it looked.

Pink Perfection, Melody Crust, 2½" × 3½". Which way is up? The beaded fringe tells the tale.

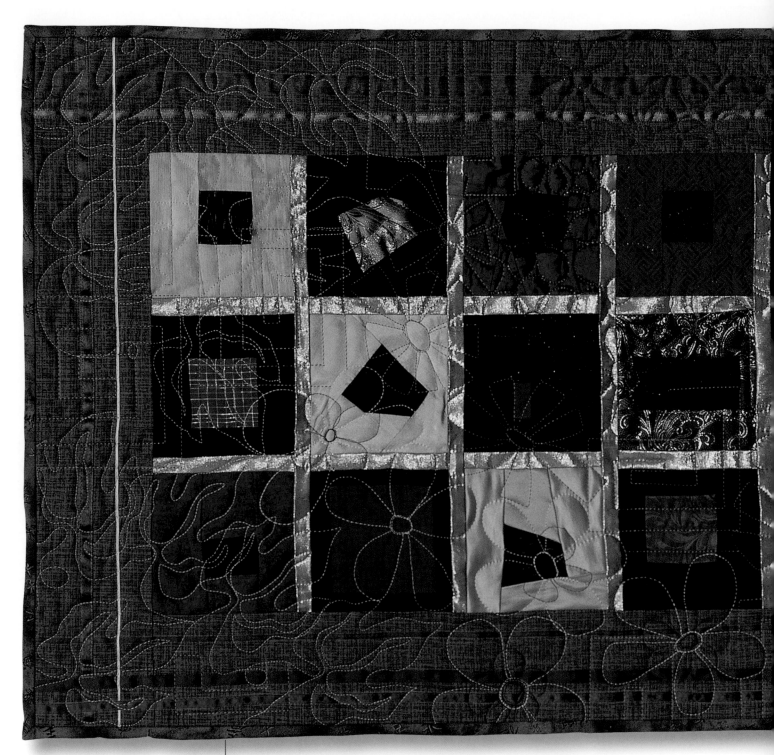

The Jewel, Melody Crust, 29″ × 20″.
*Colorful ribbon stripes in the border
serve to highlight and frame the fancy
fabrics used to piece the blocks.*

3 RIBBON, RICK RACK, AND MORE

Through the ages, **RIBBON** has been a source of **DELIGHT**. A prettily wrapped package signals treasure within, and the **FANCIER** the ribbon, the greater the **ANTICIPATION**. And ribbon is just the beginning; there is an abundance of trims ready to provide us **OPPORTUNITIES** to embellish our work. I **CHALLENGE** you to think about rickrack, bias tape, cord, fringe, doilies, and lace without feeling your **CREATIVE** urges spring to life. Old handkerchiefs or special fabrics, such as lamé, ultra-suede, or embossed velvet are other materials that can add that **SPECIAL SOMETHING** to any project. The possibilities are so exciting!

A jumble of just a few of the luscious ribbons tempting all of us.

RIBBON

Luxurious, sensuous, and colorful, ribbon takes almost anything up a notch or two. Look over your stash and find some ribbons that will work well with your project. Silk ribbons are soft and pliable enough to lend themselves to embroidery. Others are stiff and need more coaxing to stay where you want them, but can easily be attached with embroidery or beads. You can have a lot of fun adding ribbon and trim to quilts and garments using techniques other than just straight sewing.

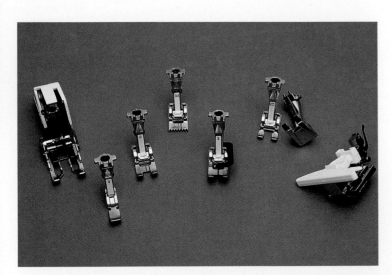

These presser feet; from left, walking foot, zipper foot, zigzag foot, pin tuck foot, edge-stitching foot, open toe foot, Ribbon Wizard, all help make the project at hand less troublesome and much more fun.

SUPPLIES CHECKLIST

✓ **RIBBON**

✓ **THREAD** Any type in contrasting or matching colors. See also page 104.

✓ **SHARP PINS** such as long silk pins

✓ **SHARP SCISSORS**

✓ **HOOP** for silk ribbon embroidery

✓ **MARKING PEN OR PENCIL** Choose one that is easily erasable.

✓ **GLUE STICK OR FUSIBLE WEB** for basting

✓ **FUSIBLE INTERFACING** for making ribbon fabric

Machine Sewing

✓ **SHARP, JEANS, OR QUILTING NEEDLE** in the smallest size possible from an assortment including #70/10, 75/11 and 80/12. (Always use a brand new needle to avoid snagging the ribbon.)

✓ **ASSORTED PRESSER FEET** Next to the needle, the presser foot used to guide the ribbon or trim is the most important tool. The best feet for the job don't just hold the ribbon down, they let you see what you are doing, too. Every machine has a different assortment of feet, so choose the best one for your needs from among them:

Couching, ruching, ribbon, fabric and three-dimensional flowers or leaves all add a dynamic texture to quilts and clothing.

Prep Work and Supplies

Keeping a wide variety of ribbons close to hand will make it possible for you to incorporate them into your quilting projects at a moment's notice. Little or no preparation is required. If you plan on laundering your finished project, however, make sure that the ribbons you select wash well. As with any new material, pre-test if you are uncertain. To avoid shrinkage or bleeding, I always recommend pre-washing ribbon before sewing it into your projects. Put the ribbon in a mesh bag and wash it by hand or machine in warm water with a mild soap. Rinse well and either hang the ribbon to dry or lay it flat. Ribbons labeled *perma-trim* or *no-iron* have been specially treated to retain their shape and character regardless of the number of washings.

Some ribbons may require special handling. After cleaning silk ribbons, a very light misting with plain water will restore their luster. Organdy can be either washed or dry-cleaned. Ribbon floss can be washed in cold (not hot) water or dry cleaned.

Ribbons, like any other fabric, are happiest when kept dust free and away from light. Some quilters store their ribbons rolled on cardboard, sorted by type and color. I'm perfectly happy to store mine in a jumble in plastic tubs. Not only am I too impatient to roll ribbon (where's the fun in that?), but as I rummage through the bins, I often come across a scrap of forgotten ribbon and am struck with a sudden inspiration on just how to incorporate it into my project.

- OPEN TOE EMBROIDERY, PIN TUCK or CORDING FOOT for narrow ribbons
- ZIGZAG or OPEN TOE EMBROIDERY FOOT for wider ribbons
- EDGE JOINING FOOT to join two lengths of ribbon together side by side
- RIBBON WIZARD OR A ZIPPER FOOT to simplify stitching one ribbon on top of another (both work well—remember to move the needle to one side, just far enough to barely catch the edge of the ribbon)

Hand Sewing

✓ CHENILLE NEEDLES for embroidering with ribbon. These have an eye large enough to accommodate the ribbon and also make a hole large enough for the ribbon to pass through the fabric without being crushed.

✓ EMBROIDERY NEEDLES a large-eye size 8 Between is a good choice for general sewing.

✓ TAPESTRY (BLUNT NOSED) NEEDLE for wrapped stitches. This is particularly important if you are adding a ribbon design to an item such as a pair of knit gloves where it's important to not puncture the yarns as you work.

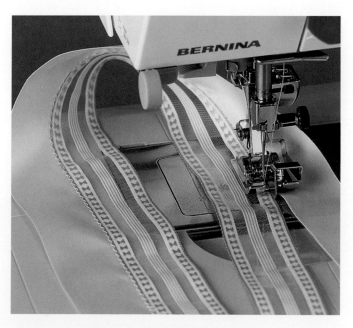

The edge-stitching foot is made especially to join two things together, including (but certainly not limited to) ribbon and fabric.

RIGHT, **Buttons, Bangles and Bows**, *Melody Crust, 28" × 28". The soft colors of this quilt serve as a suitable backdrop for some delicate and very feminine embellishments.* ABOVE, **Buttons, Bangles and Bows**, *detail. The satin ribbon ruched flower sets off the jewel beautifully, ultimately making both look more lavish.*

It Dawned On Me, *Melody Crust, 2½" × 3½". Not having the right colored ribbon is no problem! The light pink and yellow ribbons started out as white and were both painted to the exact shade I wanted.*

Ribbon Types

There are two basic types of ribbon; woven edge and cut edge. If the ribbon was woven on a loom, it will have finished edges and will be suitable for stitch-down applications. Some varieties have a thin copper wire woven into the edges. Any woven ribbon can be either sheer, printed, metallic, or patterned. Cut-edge, or craft ribbon works well for craft and floral type projects and can be glued or wired, but will crack and fray if sewn or washed.

Satin Ribbon

The word *satin* refers not to the material the ribbon is made of, but its shine. Woven-edge satin ribbons—single-face, double-face, and picot-edge—are inexpensive and can be found in most quilt shops and fabric stores. Made from 100 percent polyester, they are manufactured in a bounty of beautiful colors and come in widths varying from ¹⁄₁₆″ to 3″.

Grosgrain Ribbon

Grosgrain ribbon is closely woven cloth with heavy cross-threads and a somewhat dull finish. Widely available in both solids and prints, it's often reversible and you

Pretty Maids All in a Row, Melody Crust, 30″ × 15″. Dressing paper dolls was a favorite childhood pastime. Now I play with fabric, ribbon, buttons, and beads instead of paper.

can easily find it in widths ranging from ¼″ to 3″. Modern grosgrain is 100 percent polyester, so it generally shrinks at a rate of less than two percent. Even a small amount of shrinkage may cause it to pucker later, so pre-wash it. Grosgrain is fairly dense and works best when added to straight or very slightly curved areas.

Silk Ribbon

Very soft and pliable, silk ribbon is an ideal candidate for use in embroidery. It's readily available in 2 mm, 4 mm, and 7 mm widths and, if you are lucky, you may occasionally stumble across a source of the more unusual wider widths. Remember that the narrower the ribbon, the smaller and more delicate your work will turn out to be.

Not only does this lovely ribbon come in many colors, but there are also hand-dyed versions on the market. A polyester version of "silk" ribbon is now available. This replica has more spring and gives a slightly heavier look to your work.

Wire-Edge Ribbons

Wire in the edge of a ribbon allows it to be molded while still maintaining its shape. The edge of the material can be folded over the very thin wires. Thicker wires are typically covered with thread that matches the ribbon. Gold, silver, or iridescent thread is sometimes used, creating a ribbon known as *gold wire-edge ribbon*.

Wire-edge ribbon, with its ease of sculpture, is an excellent choice for making flowers, mainly because it's easy to gather it by pulling one of the wires. You will find that it's available in a wide variety of widths and colors, including *ombré*, meaning a ribbon shaded from light to dark.

China Cabinet, detail of label. The wire-edged ribbon, meant to replicate fine china, was gathered by pulling on just one of the wires. The gold trim adds to the china effect, and the bits of lace represent the table linens. See full quilt on page 86.

Organ>dy Ribbon

Any sheer ribbon may be labeled *organdy*. This is generally 100 percent nylon and comes in an enormous assortment of sizes and colors. Sheer ribbon is one of my favorites. I can scrunch it into any shape, and it allows me to create a three-dimensional punch that really shows up well. It's also easy to scoot with the tip of a needle and secure to projects with beads, buttons, embroidery stitches, or any other decorative element that comes to mind.

ABOVE LEFT, **Eye Candy** (*sheer ribbon*), Melody Crust, 3½" × 2½". I start with a long piece of ribbon, skooching it into place as I go. When I get to the end, I just cut the ribbon to the exact length I need. ABOVE RIGHT, **Blue Bag**, detail. A variety of ribbons intertwine for lush texture and richness. See Also page 116.

Fancy Ribbons

Jacquard is a woven, embroidered ribbon. Other fancy ribbons include metallics (meaning shiny gold, silver, or copper ribbon), velvets, ginghams, plaids, stripes, box pleats, and ribbons enhanced with pearls or lace. They're all uniquely elegant and distinctive.

Another fancy ribbon you may want to experiment with is monofilament-edge ribbon. A very thin fish-line in the ribbon edge gives it a bit of extra body, but not quite as much as a wire edge. (Another difference is that while you can

RIGHT, **Hugs and Love**, J.B. Scarf, 13" × 13". A wide free-form swath of sheer red organdy ribbon draws the eye to the charming spray of ribbon floss. There's lots of fancy stitching here, too—the heavy purple thread was stitched from the bobbin. ABOVE, Ribbons, threads and beads used to create **Hugs and Love**.

On the left are ribbons made from fabric. In the center, ribbon has been attached over ribbon or decoratively stitched with thread. The ribbons on the right have all been painted.

gather and pull the wires of wire-edge ribbon, you cannot do so with monofilament-edge ribbon.)

Ribbon Floss

A soft, braided ribbon, usually made of acrylic, ribbon floss is very pliable and, in fact, is more like thread than ribbon. Look for a variety of colors, including metallics. Ribbon floss works well for couching and in your machine's bobbin.

Hand-Made Ribbon

Many fabrics are perfect for making your own ribbon: silks, lightweight cottons, and polyesters, just to name a few. Fabrics that are too light can always be fused together. Experiment with fancy edges by using a wavy-edged rotary cutter. Use a seam sealant if your project is likely to experience heavy use. (Just remember that the seam sealant may discolor your fabric, so test a separate piece to avoid unwelcome surprises.) Stitching the edges, either by hand or machine, is definitely the most permanent preventative for possible fraying. Machine stitchers will need to use a stabilizer.

You can make wired ribbon with your sewing machine. Cut your fabric into crosswise strips and lay a length of fine wire down one edge. Turn a narrow edge over the wire and temporarily secure it with some tape. Zigzag the entire length, then repeat the process on the other side of the ribbon.

Decorated Ribbon

Who says you can't embellish an embellishment? Adorn any ribbon with coordinating or contrasting threads, beads, paint, or other ribbons and trims. Apply thread by hand or machine, using straight stitches or fancy embroidery. A permanent fabric marker can change a nondescript ribbon to a spectacular one in minutes—and in just the right color, too! Beads and buttons are best applied after the ribbon is

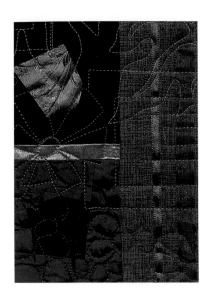

attached to the project, otherwise they can be problematic to sew around.

RIBBON APPLICATIONS

Couching

Couching involves sewing over (rather than through) a decorative ribbon, cord, or trim. Depending on your own preference, it can be stitched on one layer of fabric or through all the layers of a quilt, either by hand or machine. Use invisible thread that won't show at all or a contrasting thread to emphasize your stitching, with the ribbon providing a colorful background.

When couching by machine, arrange the ribbon in a pleasing design, then apply it with a zigzag, blind hem, or any other wide stitch. To couch by hand, take small stitches around, then under the arranged ribbon or other trim, attaching it to the fabric. These small stitches can easily include embroidery, buttons, or beads, as well.

Ruching

Ruched ribbon is tremendously impressive. The ruching allows the ribbon (or fabric) to act like a bias trim. You can shape it into flowers or any other curved shape, as well as use it in a straight line.

Start by cutting the ribbon two or three times as long as the intended finished length. Run a continuous gathering line (this is easiest done by hand with a strong thread) in a zigzag pattern along the ribbon, then pull the thread to gather. Pin the ruched ribbon to your project, then tie off the gathering thread before you sew it in place. This way, you will know for sure it's the right length before you commit yourself by knotting the thread.

Ribbon Flowers

Informal ribbon flowers are created from grosgrain or satin ribbon. Wire edged ribbon lends itself to making slightly more elegant flowers. This is a good time to experiment with a variety of ribbon textures to see what different effects you can create.

Designers will tell you that flowers arranged in odd numbered groups (three, five, seven, or nine) make an arrangement more pleasing to the eye. After nine, of course, no one will notice whether the numbers are odd or even.

Folded Rose

Folded ribbon roses add a gracious detail to any project. For ribbon ranging in width from ¼″ to ⅜″ wide, cut a 10″ length. Have a needle, threaded and knotted with a matching colored thread, ready to go. Fold the ribbon in half at a 90° angle,

ABOVE, **The Jewel**, *detail. Edge stitching sheer purple and blue satin ribbons creates a gleaming border. See full quilt on page 68.* ABOVE RIGHT, **Blue Bag**, *detail. Texture, texture and more texture is the name of the game here. See also page 116.*

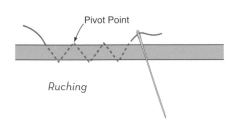

Pivot Point

Ruching

Quick Tip

Take it from me, the most important step in making a ribbon rose is having a prepared needle within easy reach. Sitting there with your folded ribbon tightly clamped between thumb and fingers is not the time to start wondering how you are going to thread a needle with your one remaining free hand!

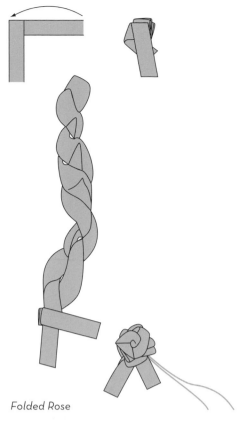

Folded Rose

Pink Purse, *detail. I intentionally left long tails on the folded ribbon flowers, knowing I wanted to attach them with more beads. Buttons or a favorite charm would work here, too. See also page 87.*

then fold the bottom over the top, one side at a time, maintaining the square shape. To finish, pinch the two ribbon tails between your fingers and thumb, then let go of the folded part. Still holding on, gently pull *one* tail to form a rose. Hand stitch up and down through the center until it is completely secure.

Rosettes

For ribbon that is ¼" wide, cut a 2½" length; ⅜" wide ribbon will need to be cut 4½" long; and cut a 1" ribbon into a 6" length. Start by folding the ribbon in half, right sides together. With small stitches, sew the short ends together and secure the thread. *Without cutting the thread tail,* make a row of small gathering stitches close to one edge. Turn the circle around so the seam is on the inside and pull the thread to gather. Still leaving the thread uncut, sew

Buttons, Bangles and Bows, *detail. Rosette supported shank buttons stay face up, instead of following their natural inclination, which is to fall sideways. See full quilt on page 72.*

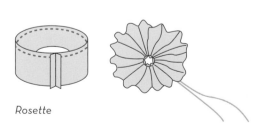

Rosette

*ABOVE LEFT, **Garland**, before. Looks a bit like a tablecloth-covered table, don't you think? ABOVE RIGHT, **Garland**, Melody Crust, 12" × 16". Now that we've put a splashy floral arrangement on top, it looks like a celebration!*

the flower onto your project, then sew a bead or button at the center, secure your thread, and cut it.

Leaves

As you might use a variety of greenery to add lushness to a floral display, look at different colors and textures of ribbon to serve the same purpose. To make leaves, cut a 2" length of ¼" ribbon; 3" of ½" ribbon; or 4" of 1" ribbon. Fold the ribbon as shown. Stitch a row of gathering stitches across the base of the leaf, pull the thread to gather, and secure the thread. Before cutting the thread, attach the leaf to your project.

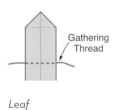

Gathering Thread

Leaf

Stems

Make beautiful ribbon stems for your flowers. Cut the ribbon the length of the finished stem and attach it by couching. You can either use a ribbon that is just the right width for your stem, or create a three-dimensional look by rolling a wider

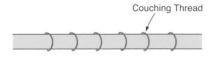

Couching Thread

Stem

ribbon into a tube shape. Either way, attach the stem by couching, using matching thread. Stitch over the ribbon at regular (or irregular) intervals, then secure the thread.

Silk Ribbon Embroidery

Start by marking your design with an erasable pen; no marking is necessary if you design as you go. Use 12″ or less silk ribbon on your needle at one time—any more and the ribbon will fray. Knot the ribbon, bring your needle up from the back, and stitch. When you are at the end of the line, pull the silk to the back of your project and secure it with a second needle and regular sewing thread. If you make a knot, as you would normally do with thread, you are almost guaranteed to unintentionally pull all of the fullness out of your ribbon, making it look flat and ordinary.

The secret to successful silk ribbon embroidery is controlling both the tension and the twist of the ribbon. Most embroidery stitches work well for this type of material, but the less tension you apply to it, the better off you will be. Pulling the ribbon taut will mean losing the decorative dimension inherent in ribbon. Use your thumb and a toothpick (this is pretty tiny stuff to be working with) to keep the ribbon relaxed and in position as you sew.

Minimizing the twist is the second secret. Ribbon has a mind of its own and it naturally wants to twist. The more you allow this to occur, the less impact your finished ribbon embroidery will have.

When applying this ribbon, remember that "wearer friendly" stitches lie flat on the fabric or are knotted, wrapped, whipped, or braided. Looped and plume stitches are best used for non-garment pieces.

Bows

Tie a bow that looks good every time by following these simple steps. First, take a piece of ribbon and form two loops. Holding a loop in each hand (they look like bunny ears at this point), tie a single knot. Instead of trying to stick out at odd angles, your tails will both be pointed down.

Now that you have made a great bow, be as creative as you want to be in how you attach it. You might decide to leave the tails very long (4″ to 10″) and attach them with beads, buttons, French knots, or any other decorative embroidery. Or you could add your bows when you are machine tacking your quilt in order to create a particularly delicate look.

Ribbon Fabric

You can make your own one-of-a-kind fabric, using just ribbon by basket-weaving any woven-edge ribbons over a colored or black background. (It might be easier to use a fusible interfacing rather than a fabric background—the fusible will help stabilize the ribbon for later sewing.) Pin the ribbons in place, then sew them down. Use this "fabric" any way you would use any other material—but wouldn't it look fabulous as a basket on an appliqué quilt?

Pretty Maids All in a Row, detail. This silk ribbon application seemed like the perfect way to dress up my doll. See full quilt on page 73.

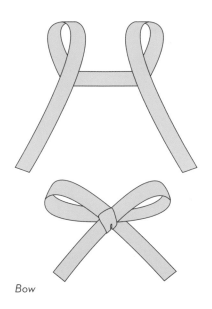

Bow

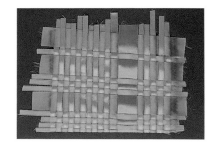

You can combine colors, sizes, and textures of ribbon to make your own eye-popping fabric.

RIGHT, **New Year's Eve**, Melody Crust, 23" × 23". Lots of different ribbon applications here; couching, flowers, and bows, just to mention a few. Beads, buttons, and various other embellishments are also well represented. ABOVE, **New Year's Eve**, detail. Note the hand-couched ribbons and the silk and rayon ribbon embroidery

Basting

Admittedly, basting is an extra step when working with ribbon, but it really does ensure faster, easier, and more accurate placement when you are sewing. There are a number of basting methods: thread, glue stick or fusible web. To thread-baste, make long stitches using a small needle and fine thread, preferably in a contrasting color for easy removal. Either fine silk or cotton thread works well here because neither will leave large holes in a delicate ribbon. Glue stick is a good water-soluble basting alternative. It can be a bit messy, but doesn't change the hand of your project. Fusible web is available in ¼" and ½" widths or you can cut any width you need from yardage. The web is applied with an iron, to the ribbon, per the manufacturer's instructions, and then the ribbon is ironed directly onto your project. This permanent application stiffens the hand of the item, but certainly makes top-stitching very easy.

Sewing with Ribbon

Many a project has been subject to a radical last minute redesign because of a shortage of just a few inches of ribbon, so always allow a little more than you think you will need. It's also important to keep the ribbon in a relaxed position when handling it, even when you are stitching it in place. If you pull it taut, it will relax after sewing and cause puckering.

When you are attaching narrow ribbons (⅛″ or narrower) to fabric, sew one row of stitches down the center. Wider ribbons will stay in place nicely if you sew a row of stitches along each edge. Sewing along both edges in the same direction, using a medium length straight stitch, blind hem, or blanket stitch, will also help prevent puckering. When you are placing ribbon within or along a seam, first stitch it on one side and then sew your seam, catching up the other.

If you want to disguise your stitches, use a matching colored thread, or use contrasting thread to highlight them. Use a toothpick to put a light application of any seam sealant to cut edges to prevent fraying.

Care of Ribbon Projects

If laundering your finished project is likely to happen, pre-wash the ribbon to prevent future shrinking or bleeding (see page 26). All garments should always be turned inside out. Carefully pressing around any ribbons or placing them on a thick towel and lightly steaming, will ensure the best results. After cleaning projects that include silk ribbon, a very light misting with plain water will restore the ribbon's luster.

RICK RACK, BIAS TAPE, TRIM, CORDS, AND TASSELS

To put it in New York City terms, ribbon may be the Upper East Side, but there are plenty of good times to be had in the other boroughs! Rick rack and bias tape have long been favorites for good reason—they are colorful, easy to handle, and durable. Cords of all sizes are easy to make and add a spectacular touch to any project, and tassels are in an elegant class all their own.

Purchased trims of all types can be used to decorate your quilts and garments. Trims are great for decorating vases on floral appliqué, as the focus of crazy quilt blocks, or as a special touch on an art quilt. Manufacturers are wracking their imaginations coming up with new trim ideas every day, so by all means, let your imagination fly to new ways to use them!

Prep Work and Supplies

Embellishments like rick rack, cords, and other trims are readily available in fabric shops and craft stores. They need little special treatment before adding to your projects. As with other embellishments, read the manufacturer's instructions before using them. If

Eye Candy with eyelash trim, *Melody Crust, 3½″ × 2½″. Fuzzy eyelash yarn lends this small quilt a dash of buoyancy.*

Blue Bag, *detail. In my search for spots to add more stuff, I noticed this rick rack. The ins and outs are perfect places for buttons, beads and stitching. See also page 116.*

you are still uncertain, take time to test that they are washable before committing to them (see page 26). No special materials, beyond basic sewing supplies, are needed.

Rick Rack

Rick rack, perhaps the boldest of all trims, comes in three sizes, many of which are color coordinated. Baby rick rack is a perfect accent for miniature projects. Medium-sized rick rack is great for flowers and most clothing needs, whether inserted in a seam or sewn flat on top. Jumbo rick rack makes a very bold statement and somewhat larger flowers. Generally speaking, the larger the rick rack, the stiffer the hand, although 100 percent cotton (usually vintage) rick rack is delightfully soft and pliable.

Use one color to complement your project or several coordinated colors for a fun, bright look. You will find that rick rack is easy to work with because the edges don't curl.

If you are gathering rick rack into flowers, vary the size of the finished posies by your choice of rick rack size, length of trim or the tightness of the gathering. And be sure to use a heavy thread when gathering sturdy rick rack, so it won't try to break on you. To glue-baste rick rack, apply glue dots (white fabric glues that come with a tiny applicator tip are the best choice) under each point, then simply place it in position.

Inserting Rick Rack into Seams

Pin the rick rack at the seam line so that half of it is on the outside of the seam line and the other half is lying inside it. Baste the rick rack in place, stitching on your intended seam line. Turn the fabric over, wrong side up, on top of the second piece and pin the two together, matching up the seam lines. Sew the fabric pieces together on the stitching line.

Sewing Rick Rack Flat

To machine sew, pin the rick rack into position and stitch along the center. To sew it by hand, use small stitches and a strong thread and sew down each side of the rick rack at the outermost point. Variations might include adding a bead at each stitch, adding a bead in each valley, or adding beads in both places. Buttons can also be relied upon to add a festive touch.

Bias Tape

Bias tapes are used to bind raw edges or to make borders on clothes and quilts. Because bias tape has the ability to curve and turn corners easily, it's a great ready-to-use trim. You can make sewing go much faster along rounded edges by just pre-shaping the tape with your iron. Available in cotton or rayon, you will find that it comes in a large variety of widths, styles and colors.

You can also make your own bias tape from bias-cut fabric strips. The most efficient way is to use a bias tape maker. The bias strips are fed through the tool and as the folded strips come out the other end, you set the creases with a hot iron. Bias tape makers are available in a variety of sizes. You can make bias tape without this handy tool, but it's tedious work and difficult to maintain a precisely even width. How ever you make the tape, it's a good idea to spray starch your fabric before cutting it into strips.

To make this fusible bias tape fabric, I cut 1½" squares, ironed them to fusible interfacing and covered the edges with off-the-shelf fusible bias tape.

Fusible Bias Tape

This ribbon-like material comes in various widths and a multitude of colors, including shiny metallics. It's pre-folded and has an iron-on fusible web on the back. Because it is cut on the bias, it's perfect for all sorts of applications that require lots of bending and shaping, including stained glass and elaborate Celtic designs.

Fringe

Try adding off-the-shelf fringe for a refreshing touch. Depending on your design, fringe can be added to the edge or sewn into a seam. Adding fringe to the edge is done by top-stitching it into place. Stitch it on directly over the binding and miter the corners for a nice looking finish. Another technique is to pin the fringe to the edge of the quilt top, line up the edges, and machine baste it with a scant ¼" seam. Finish the edge with either a traditional binding or turn the backing under for a faced edge. These same techniques can also be used to add fringe to other parts of your project.

Cords

Cords are wonderful additions to your embellishing repertoire. They can be used to outline an important element in your design, to add extra depth and dimension or just because they are fun. Can't find just the right one for your project? No problem—it's really simple to wind your own!

Making a custom cord is a fast, fun and easy path to instant gratification. Just choose any combination of ribbon, yarn, or thread and twist them together. A Custom Corder speeds the process, but a power drill from your toolbox works just as well. I can even wind short cords using the bobbin winder on my sewing machine.

LEFT, Machine-couched cord elegantly secures the edges of this free-form shape. The tassel is a cheerful way to end the cord. BELOW, A couple of cord winders and some sample cords, along with the raw materials that make them.

Generally speaking, the length of the finished cord will be one-third the length of the raw materials you use, although this can vary a bit, depending on the thickness of the finished cord. You can customize it to suit any project. A one color, multicolor, or striped cord can easily be wound, just by choosing different raw materials.

Make about a 2" loop of thread and tie it to the side hole of a bobbin. Gather together the materials to be wound. Place them through the looped thread and insert the bobbin on its winder. Hold the ends of the loose materials tightly and turn the winder on. Twist the cord until it kinks, weigh it down in the middle, and the cord will twist together the same as above.

Making Your Own Cord

To make your own cord, you will need a hand cord winder or a power drill fitted with a small cup hook in the chuck, some sort of small weight (mine is about three ounces, attached to a hook), and basic raw materials—thread, ribbon, yarn, or whatever else suits your mood. Decide how long you want your finished cord to be and cut the threads at least three times that measurement. To make a thick trim, use either more or thicker threads. Knot the thread ends together at each end, secure one end to something sturdy, and place the other in the winder. Wind the corder clockwise or push the start button of your power drill. (Power tools running at high speed tend to startle some people, so I suggest you start at the slowest speed setting.) When the thread becomes tight enough to kink, place your weight in the center of the length of twisted cord and bring the two ends together. The two halves of the twisted cord will wind together. Remove the weight and you're done! To prevent the cord from unraveling, just tie an overhand knot at the end.

Winding short cords with your sewing machine's bobbin winder is easy. If you want to wind long ones, you will need a helper to hold the ends while you operate your machine.

Tassels

Purchased or hand-made tassels give an appealing flourish to any quilt, garment, or accessory. Used as a zipper pull or on a quilt's corner, they add an exotic touch. Tassels are easy to make to suit your exact specifications. They can be long or short, fat or thin, or anything in between. Making your own is sure to be much more affordable than buying them, assuming you can even find the color, texture, and shape that your project design calls for!

To make a simple tassel, gather together any ribbons, threads, or yarns you want to incorporate. Tassels that include bulking material (such as perle cotton or yarn)

Tassels can be made from a variety of materials, some of which are shown here.

are going to be heftier and more substantial. Wind selected materials around a piece of cardboard (the width of the cardboard will determine the tassel's length) or just gather a bundle of strands in your hand. Trim one end, then wrap the other end with a simple wrap knot. To make a wrap knot, make a loop in the wrapping cord and lay it on the gathered materials with the loose end left very long. Start wrapping the threads on the side farthest away from the loop (that is, wrap toward the loop). These wraps need to be as tight as possible. When you reach the end of the wrap, slip the end through the loop, let go of the short end, and pull on the long one. The loop will pull the ends under the wraps. Trim both ends and voila! You've made a tassel!

Wrap knot

Caring for Trim-Embellished Projects

Rick rack and bias tape are both very hard workers who ask for no special care in return. Commercially made trims are colorfast, pre-shrunk, and ready to go. If you make your own bias tape it's a simple matter to just pre-wash it the same way you will launder your project. There is such huge variability in the materials used to make other trims, tassels and cords that there is no general cleaning rule to follow. Your best bet is to start with the gentlest possible technique, such as hand washing in a mild soap and cold water, before you try more rigorous cleaning methods.

EMBELLISHING WITH FABRIC

Cloth doilies, handkerchiefs, and laces provide gracious ornamentation to any project. Happily both old and new are available in all kinds of different shapes, weights, and designs.

Another interesting way to add texture to your project is to include non-cotton fabrics. I will use any fabric that I like on my never-to-be-washed quilts, no matter the content, preferring fabrics that are about the same weight as cotton. Lightweight fabrics can be made the right weight by ironing an interfacing on to the back—my favorite is woven interfacing.

Specific fabrics tend to produce particular results—silk is lustrous, velvet always adds richness, and metallic fabrics shimmer and shine.

Prep Work and Supplies

Once you have seen the wonderful special effects you can achieve with special fabrics, you'll find yourself collecting them everywhere you go—from fabric shops to craft stores to white elephant stores and consignment shops. You need no special materials to work with them, other than your regular sewing supplies.

Often made of cotton, doilies and handkerchiefs are usually safe to machine wash and also tend to hold up well to dry cleaning. Because the fiber content of laces varies so widely, you need to be certain that you test each one for washability before you integrate it into your designs.

Neptune's Weave, *detail. This seahorse was just too small for traditional appliqué. The yellow ultra-suede worked just right and set off the beads beautifully, too! See full quilt on page 49.*

China Cabinet, *Melody Crust,*
30" × 15". My china cabinet may
be imaginary, but it has real doilies
hanging from its shelf.

Cotton velvet is machine washable and dryer safe and can even be pressed on the nap pile side. Non-cotton velvets are dry clean only and must be pressed on a needle board. A needle board looks like a large pet brush and sits flat on the ironing surface. It prevents the nap from being crushed as you iron.

Lamés can usually be machine washed on the gentle cycle (no bleach) and drip dried. If necessary, press them gently with a cool iron because too much heat can easily damage them. Always be sure to check the fabric care instructions because some lamés are dry clean only. Dry cleaning is recommended for all fused lamé fabric.

Silk care information usually states that it should be dry cleaned, but pre-washed silk won't shrink any more after the first washing. It should be noted that silk fabrics are *not* reliably colorfast, so be careful how and where you use them.

Doilies

When adding a doily to your work, be sure to secure it very well in order to prevent snagging. Cut edges can be easily dealt with by sewing them into seams. Old doilies, often found in thrift stores and at yard sales, may have a stained or discolored section that you can easily cut out and still work the remaining pieces into your design.

Handkerchiefs

Hankies, especially old ones, add a soft, feminine touch. They are an amazing source of beautiful tatting, crocheted edges, and fancy monograms.

There are so many ways to assimilate handkerchiefs into a quilt. Use the edge or the corner of an embroidered hankie for crazy quilting. Sew the cut edge into a seam and let the fancy part overlay your fabric. If a hankie seems very delicate, fuse a light

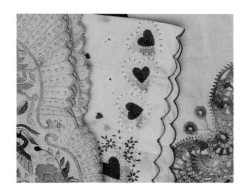

Silk and cotton hankies from my
collection are just waiting for the right
project to come along and claim them.

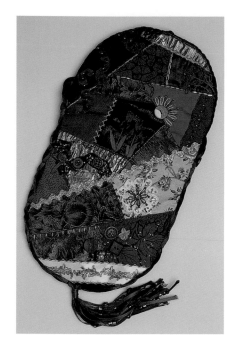

woven interfacing to it prior to cutting and piecing. In order to show off any fancy edges, consider top stitching hankies to plain blocks.

To make pretty and unique baskets, cut dainty embroidered or printed handkerchiefs in half and appliqué them onto a background fabric. Use snippets of lace to trim the basket and pieces of rickrack or bias tape to form the handles.

Believe it or not, men's handkerchiefs—often with intricate geometric patterns—also lend themselves to basket making. Cut one into fourths, trim it with bits and pieces of whatever suits your fancy, and make bias tape handles. For easier sewing, stabilize handkerchiefs with very lightweight iron-on interfacing, then selectively cut and sew them into your favorite piecing pattern.

Lace

Laces are often made from a blend of fibers, ranging from durable to very fragile. Lace trims that come by the yard are made from cotton or cotton blends and are very amenable to being topstitched or stitched into seams.

Inexpensive machine-woven laces have quite a bit of open space incorporated into them, giving them a light and airy look. Lace yardage sometimes comes with either a shiny or a matte fabric lining. In this case, both lace and lining are used as one trim. If the backing fabric contrasts with the lace, the pattern will show very distinctly; if it's a close match in color, the lace pattern will subtly blend in with it.

Velvet

All velvets are not alike. They differ a great deal in feel, drape-ability, handling, sewing, and care. Velvet can be made from cotton, silk, rayon, or a combination of rayon and acetate. The nap, or pile, affects how you will want to handle the fabric in several ways. The color of the fabric changes dramatically, depending on the direction of the pile. If you are working with patchwork, this color difference can be an advantage. If you are using the velvet in several places in your quilt top and want it all to look the same, be careful that you piece all of it with the nap going in the same direction. Quilting on velvet barely shows, if at all, because the shadows that quilting normally makes are lost in the fabric's pile.

Embossing Velvet

Embossing velvet is quick and simple and can make a very dramatic addition to many projects, including crazy quilting, scarves, and throw pillows. Choose a rubber stamp and lay it face-up on your ironing board. Lay a piece of rayon velvet face down over the stamp and mist the fabric with water. Cover it with a press

LEFT, **Pink Purse**, Melody Crust. What better place to apply pretty bits and pieces than to a lady's fancy purse? ABOVE, **Pink Purse**, detail. I thought the motif of this lace appliqué was perfect, but it was so light it looked a little stark against the colorful background. Embroidering the center in a color picked up from the background created harmony among all of the parts.

Embossed velvet offers endless dramatic design possibilities.

cloth, set your dry iron on the wool setting and then lift-and-press the iron evenly over the surface for about ten seconds. The stamp design will appear to be embossed into the velvet. Try this technique on velveteen, velour, and other piled fabrics. For the best results, adjust your iron temperature to meet the requirements of the particular fabric you are working with. To turn your embossed motif into an iron-on applique, add a piece of fusible web face-down onto the stack, just before you cover the velvet with the press cloth.

Lamé Fabrics

Lamé is an elegant material that lights up any project, but these shiny, metallic fabrics, usually made of nylon and polyester require some special handling.

Tissue lamé is very thin and ravels extremely easily. For strength and ease of handling, it should be backed with pre-shrunk fusible woven-cotton interfacing. Using an interfacing that has not been pre-shrunk or ironing it on with too hot an iron causes bubbles. With the addition of the interfacing, the lamé is about the same weight as 100 percent cotton fabric.

There are a couple of other ways to tame your lamé into submission. One is to use seam sealant on all of the cut edges. The sealant will discolor the fabric, so this is most effective when the fabric is to be pieced. Another way is to cut your lamé on the bias. Bias cut lamé, for reasons of its own, doesn't ravel.

Tricot-backed lamé has some very specific challenges, but is super-shiny and therefore often worth the extra handling it demands. It comes with backing straight from the manufacturer. This backing does not stabilize the fabric but does prevent raveling. Tricot lamé absolutely requires the use of a pressing cloth during ironing.

Silk

Silk is an elegant fabric that adds luster and richness to any project. Both the thin China silk and the thicker silk noil can be painted with great success. Silk is very sensitive to being pierced, so keep in mind that any holes left by pins and needles will likely show in your finished project. Heavier weight silks can be sewn and handled just like cottons, but you will probably want to back lighter weight ones with iron-on cotton interfacing.

Polyesters

Heavier cotton-polyester blends are fabrics I choose not to work with because they are not worth the effort it takes to fight with them. Having said that, I will also say that the lighter weight polyesters are fun to use and become manageable if you back them with interfacing or iron them with a heavy dose of spray starch.

Spotlight, detail. Shiny lamé fabrics add plenty of zing. See full quilt on page 43.

Tricot backed lamé lets the light shine through these inviting church windows.

There are so many luscious fabrics to consider, such as silk yardage, silk or polyester scarves from a thrift store, or these hand-dyed damask linens.

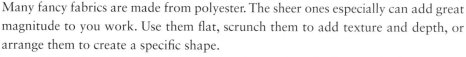

LEFT, **Garden Party**, Melody Crust, 20″ × 20″. There might not have been a party at all if not for these beautiful sheer polyesters that were just begging to dance. ABOVE, **Garden Party**, detail. The iris looks rich because of the layers. As you can see, the fabrics are all heat-cut. The real interest here is the depth of stitching—layers upon layers of fabric, French knots, and beads.

This old solder iron got a new lease on life in my studio. I use it to heat cut polyester and silk fabrics that are prone to ravel, thus stopping them in their tracks.

Many fancy fabrics are made from polyester. The sheer ones especially can add great magnitude to you work. Use them flat, scrunch them to add texture and depth, or arrange them to create a specific shape.

Handling these fabrics can pose some interesting challenges, the biggest one being that they like to ravel. Burning the edges rather than cutting them can keep this from getting out of control. Heating the fabric melts the fiber ends into small globs and fuses all the ends together. An old soldering iron is a handy tool for this process. In my experience, it's easier if you tape the fabric onto a piece of pressboard or fiberboard first, then carefully burn the "cuts."

If you find it helpful, you can put a template under a piece of glass (for safety's sake, tape the edges of the glass) and cut any shape you want. Be sure to work in a well-ventilated area, as this process can create a bit of a stink.

Ultra-suede

This synthetic suede fabric is easy to work with, machine washable, and the luscious colors are permanent. One of its greatest claims to fame is that it doesn't ravel, but it also doesn't feed particularly well through sewing machines, so use a walking foot for stitching. Decorative threads and fancy stitches show up well against ultra-suede, so think about using this fabric when your design calls for a very small appliqué.

Neptune's Weave, detail. A fish all dressed up in its fanciest fabric tail! See full quilt on page 49.

Consider using Prairie Points to give your quilts a different finish or perhaps an added three-dimensional bounce. They can be sewn at the outer edge of a quilt or inserted into a seam and are equally effective when used in garments.

Vary the look of your Prairie Points by using more than one fabric or more than one size: the squares for the Prairie Points, cut from different fabrics, are either 2″, 2½″ or 4″. The spacing is deliberately uneven.

THREE DIMENSIONAL EFFECTS

Never one to overlook an opportunity to add depth and texture to my work, I know that I can fold, pleat, and gather a variety of fabrics to add another dimension to my work. The following techniques can be accomplished with virtually any fabric.

Prairie Points

To make a Prairie Point, cut a fabric square (your point will end up being one quarter the size of the original square). Fold it in half diagonally to make a triangle and press, then fold the triangle in half again, align the raw edges, and press again. You will get much crisper folds if you spray your fabric with starch.

Starting in the corner, pin each Prairie Point to the edge of your quilt top, aligning raw edges as you go. Arrange the points so the spacing is even and machine baste, using a scant ¼″ seam allowance. For easier sewing, be sure to place the open sides of the folded points away from your presser foot.

Back and quilt your layers together, then trim your backing fabric to ½″. Turn the points out and press the seam allowance under. (If you want to reduce the bulk, trim your batting in the seam allowance.) Lastly, fold the edge of the backing under and hand stitch it down.

Fabric Ruching

Ruching with fabric is just taking a flat strip of material and hand sewing it edge to edge with a straight stitch following a zigzag pattern. Use a strong thread so that it won't break when you gather the fabric to whatever tightness you prefer. (See drawing on page 76.)

Don't overlook plaid or striped fabrics; just remember that the pivot point is more critical if you want to make the most of your fabric pattern. Make a practice piece so you know in advance that your fabric will show to its best advantage.

Gathered Fabric

To machine sew with gathers, install the gathering foot onto your sewing machine. Cut a test strip and sew it, changing the relationship of the stitch length and thread tension until you find one that you particularly like. You can also play with the adjustment of the gathering foot, itself. Cut another strip of fabric exactly 12″ long, gather it, and then measure the finished length. Using this sewn test strip, it's easy to approximate how long to cut the fabric strip in order to fit it to your design.

Finished edges can be pinked or hemmed with either a straight or decorative stitch. The thread can match or contrast and you might choose to cut the strips using a wavy edge rotary cutter, in which case there is no need to hem at all.

Gathering shows up very well because it creates bold shadows in the hills and valleys. Solid and light colored fabrics highlight the gathers most dramatically. These ruffles can be added to your project by sewing down the center, adding them into a seam, or stitching them on both sides.

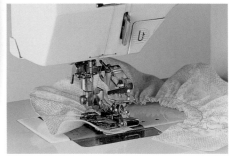

The gathering foot is a device that is very simple to use. The gathers are held in place because the stitches are secure. A long stitch and tight tension setting makes the fullest gathering; with a shorter stitch and lower tension, the fullness decreases. For additional variations, play with different tension settings while maintaining the same stitch length.

Yo-Yos

Yo-yos are an effective use of fabric scraps. They make great flowers and interesting edges on a quilt or garment and are easily attached with blind decorative stitches. A 2½″ cut circle makes about a 1¼″ yo-yo.

Make a circle template—a 2½″ round is a good size to start. Using the template, cut your fabric. Thread the needle with a strong thread and knot the end. Turn under ⅛″ at the edge of each circle and do a running stitch very close to the folded edge. Draw the thread tightly to form a yo-yo, then secure the thread ends. Arrange the yo-yos on your project, tacking each one separately (this allows you to move any single yo-yo later if you decide to reposition it).

IDEA GALLERY

You and I both **KNOW** that you have spools and snippets of ribbon **STASHED** away here, there, and elsewhere. Don't you think now is a great **TIME** to get them out and start **PLAYING**? Perhaps one of these **EXAMPLES** is just the inspiration you need.

A paper mache box bought at a craft store and covered with polka dot ribbon. Add a few appliqués glued on top and you are sure to wow the recipient of a fancy birthday box.

Ruched ribbon stems and leaves add vigor to an appliqué flower.

Eye Candy, ribbon binding, Melody Crust, 2½" × 3½". The binding is formed by half-inch satin ribbon fused onto the piece.

Eye Candy, trim edge, Melody Crust, 2½" × 3½". Yellow and green flowers are framed by green binding and yellow trim. The striped background fabric is deliberately skewed to create the feeling of movement.

Cords are very versatile. They can make a border either formal or playful, depending on how you lay them out.

IDEA GALLERY

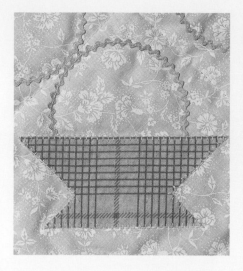

Small rickrack stitched down the middle makes dainty basket handles.

Stitching done on ultra-suede sits right on top, making each and every stitch really stand out.

Striped cords: join two colors of raw materials together by knotting the ends together. Position the knots in the center of the loop and wind the cord as described on page 84. Once you hang your weight in the center, the cord will wrap itself into a two-colored striped beauty.

Never one to miss an opportunity to incorporate beads, I slipped some pretty ones into these cords during the twisting process.

Pretty Maids All in a Row, *detail of label. Doilies and other leftovers come together to make a charming label. See full quilt on page 73.*

Sunstream, Melody Crust, 2½" × 3½". *Machine-stitched rick rack is further embellished with beads.*

Camille, Melody Crust, 2½" × 3½". *The flower makes a strong statement, so the leaf needs to be extra lustrous in order stand up for itself.*

Chatty Blossoms, Melody Crust,
41" × 63". Cotton, rayon, metallic
threads, and lots of couching all add to
this quilt's lushness.

4 THREAD PLAY!

The minute the first item of **CLOTHING** was fashioned by some ancient ancestor, I imagine someone looked at it and thought, "A few **DECORATIVE** stitches would make that so much more attractive!" So it comes as no surprise that needles made of bone or ivory were one of the first **TOOLS** man (or woman) invented. The ability to sew warm clothing made it possible for **PEOPLE** to stop their nomadic search for warmer climates and, even better, gave generations of seamstresses a new arena in which to express their **CREATIVITY**. Thread may have once been considered a basic necessity of sewing, but happily it now comes in so many luscious **COLORS** and types that it has become sheer pleasure to use. You owe it to yourself to explore some of the delicious **DESIGN** options inherent in thread. Using the right tools at the right time allows you to focus attention on the fun, creative part of the **SEWING** process. Knowing which thread or needle produces what result will lead you naturally down new paths of **EMBELLISHMENT**.

TOP LEFT, *Fairyland*, Melody Crust, 56" × 35". Machine quilting through the layers changes the visual impact of an entire quilt. TOP RIGHT, *Fairyland*, top prior to quilting. ABOVE, *Fairyland*, detail. What a difference your choice of thread can make!

MACHINE STITCHING

Sewing machines are like puppies. If you understand their inherent capabilities and gently coax them to behave, you will enjoy a calm and satisfying lifelong relationship. On the other hand, if you try to force them into behaviors that violate their basic natures, you may find yourself saddled with an ill-mannered and uncooperative beast that infuriates you at every turn. Believe me when I say that time given to learning how to work with your machine instead of against it will pay off handsomely in many, many of hours of trouble-free and productive sewing.

Prep Work and Supplies

Most of the information you need when you begin embellishing by machine you have already learned from earlier sewing experiences or is available in your sewing machine manual. Beyond threads and needles, the only essential is practice—and a little patience.

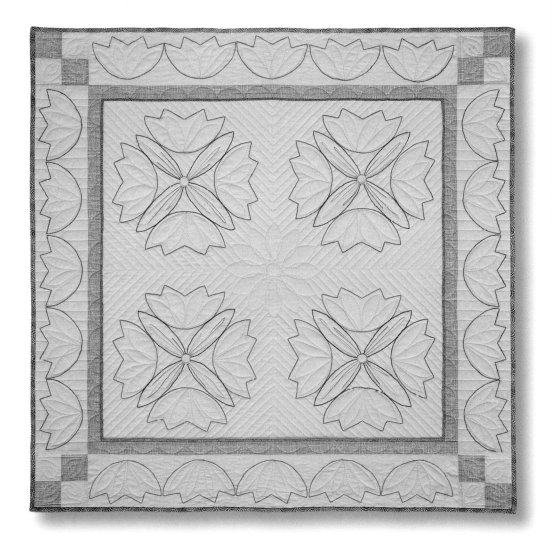

LEFT, **Clematis**, Melody Crust, 40" × 40". Clematis is all about thread. An old applique pattern suggested the design, which was outlined with three strands of orange and green embroidery thread. ABOVE RIGHT, **Clematis**, detail. The "come and go" of the green thread adds to the realism of the leaves.

Selecting Machine Threads

What kind of thread should you use for machine stitching? Any thread that you can one way or another get through the machine, of course! And if the thread doesn't go through the needle, you can always put it in the bobbin and stitch from the back side instead!

When embellishing by machine, which includes everything from embroidery to quilting, you can use pretty much anything that appeals to you. The one exception is cotton hand-quilting thread, which is covered with a coating that can damage your machine's tension disks.

Always buy the best thread you can find. Inexpensive cotton thread is full of lint, which tends to build up and cause skipped or uneven stitches, thread breakage, inaccurate tension, and excessive wear and tear to the needle, the machine, and *you*. When sewing with any cotton thread you will have better results if you routinely clean your machine.

Somehow the notion seems to have evolved that the color of the bobbin thread should match the fabric on the back of your quilt. Not true! Quilting is a very important element of the overall design, so feel free to use a contrasting thread. And you might also want to keep in mind that machine quilting is much more fun when you don't have to worry about the bobbin thread peeking through to the top. This just won't be an issue if you choose to use the same color thread through both the needle and the bobbin.

There are so many standards of thread measurement that it's difficult to keep them straight. The most common methods are weight, denier, and Tex (weight in grams per 1000 meters of thread). Fortunately many manufacturers are now moving to the Tex system as a universal way of identifying thread weight. To simplify any confusion, just think about thread in terms of *light-*, *medium-*, and *heavy-weight*.

Light-weight: Tex 10 to 24
Medium-weight: Tex 27 to 35
Heavy-weight: Tex 40 to 90

When choosing thread, use both your eyes and fingers. Look at the thread, feel it, and choose the type that will provide the results you want. Remember that one of the most overlooked properties when choosing thread is its *value* (the lightness or darkness of the thread). Do you want the thread to "pop" or just to add texture? Trust your senses when you decide.

PLEASE ADD ONE LINE TO THIS PAGE

ABOVE LEFT, **Tart Sweet**, *Melody Crust, 39″ × 51″. Quilting with a number of different threads livens up any project.* ABOVE RIGHT, **Tart Sweet**, *detail. When I get bored I change the type or color of thread on top. And yes, I changed the bobbin color every time I switched colors. I would rather do that than deal with the bobbin thread when it wants to poke through to the top.*

Thread Facts

✓ **SPUN THREADS** are spun into single strands and then twisted together. Spun thread has a fuzzy look and some degree of lint. It lacks the strength of filament thread. Cotton is a spun thread. Polyester can be made into a spun thread in order to give it the appearance of cotton.

✓ **FILAMENT THREADS** are made from multiple, continuous strands of rayon, polyester, or nylon that are then twisted together to form the thread. It has the advantage of having little or no lint.

✓ **TWIST** is simply the number of turns put in the thread. Thread is twisted from multiple strands, usually two or three strands at a time. Thread made for sewing on a sewing machine should have a final Z twist pattern. Some hand-quilting threads have a final S twist. Manufacturers don't always mark their thread with the twist pattern so if you aren't sure which one you have, don't worry overmuch about it. Although it's nice to know, it isn't critical to successful sewing.

✓ **CORE THREADS** have spun cotton or spun polyester staple fibers wrapped around a polyester core. This thread has all of the disadvantages of both polyester and cotton. It stretches and is covered with lint. I recommend avoiding it.

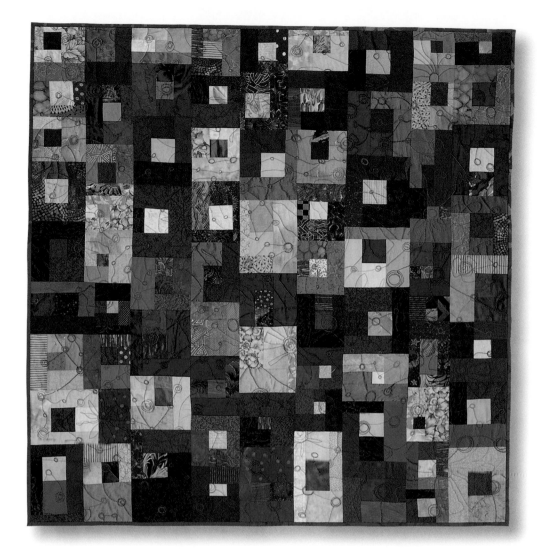

LEFT, *Fear No Color*, Melody Crust, 40" × 40". Having a working knowledge of thread types and their properties lets you bypass the struggle and jump straight to the fun. ABOVE RIGHT, *Fear No Color*, detail. The huge variety of threads, all red, not only adds unity to the quilting design, but also makes the process go faster. The quilting on this whole project took about three hours.

From the Spool to the Needle

There are two ways thread is wound on a spool—it is either *cross-wound* or *straight-wound*. Straight-wound spools work best when placed on a vertical spool pin that allows it to rotate as the thread unwinds. Be sure that the slot cut into the spool edge for fastening the loose thread end is facing toward the top.

Cross-wound spools look like the thread was wound in a figure × formation. These spools prefer to have a horizontal spool pin that allows the thread to wind off the top rather than spinning it.

Larger spools are becoming more common and are considerably more economical in the long run than standard-size spools. Cone-shaped spools have a large opening in the base and don't fit on most home sewing machines. The thread on these spools is cross-wound and is meant to pull off over the top of the spool. The easiest way to achieve this is to use an inexpensive thread stand.

When changing threads, it's better for your machine if you cut the thread at the spool and gently remove the entire length by pulling it out through the needle.

Wrapping thread spools with vinyl is a great way to keep loose ends tidy.

Storing Machine Threads

Thread, like fabric, prefers to be stored in gentle conditions; a cool, dust free place out of direct sunlight. I store my thread the way my friend, fiber artist Elizabeth Hendricks, stores hers—in a thread rack with a blackout fabric curtain to cover it when not in use.

An easy way to store spools of thread that don't already have a slot designed to secure the loose end is to cut clear vinyl strips as wide as the spools are long. Buy

Thread Types

✓ **COTTON** is the only 100 percent natural fiber thread made especially for sewing machines. It is probably the easiest of all threads to use and has certainly withstood the test of time. Cotton is available in a huge variety of colors and sizes ranging from very thin to very thick. It can be a bit linty, so clean your machine frequently when using it.

✓ **POLYESTER THREADS** are synthetically produced from polymer resins. Spun polyester is made from fiber staples spun together. It looks like cotton and it's as easy to sew with as polyester. Filament polyester is a continuous fiber thread. These opaque strands are smooth and lint free. Trilobal polyester is a multiple filament, twisted, high-sheen continuous fiber thread that looks like rayon or silk. Polyester is available in a broad range of colors. Sizes range from very thin to very thick. It offers the advantages of strength, durability, and color fastness and can have either a matte or a sheen finish. Most polyester threads are virtually lint free.

the vinyl as yardage and use an old rotary cutter (one that you have dedicated to paper cutting) to cut the strips. Then cut pieces from the strip long enough to wrap around the spool with a bit of overlap. The vinyl clings to itself and leaves no residue. Cutting long lengths of vinyl and taping them to the back of my studio door makes them easily accessible when needed.

Selecting Machine Needles

Thread passes through the eye of the needle up to 50 times before the stitch is completed, obviously making the choice of needle crucial to the stitch quality of any sewing machine.

A machine needle needs to be changed frequently. How often depends on the type of use and the skill of the operator. For example, when machine-piecing, a needle may last the length of the project—perhaps twenty hours or so. If the project is free-motion work, then the skill of the user comes into play. A skillful stitcher who can ebb and flow with the machine may use the same needle for eight to ten hours. Novices may need to change needles after only two hours because they are more likely to fight with their machines and can very easily bend the needle. In any case, the needle needs to be changed whenever the top thread shreds or breaks, when the needle makes a punching sound when piercing the fabric, or when the machine starts to skip or make uneven stitches.

I store one color of thread per shelf and sort types from left to right: flat film polyester, metallic, rayon and silk, synthetic, heavy cotton, regular weight cotton, and, finally, cotton machine embroidery thread. Avid fabric artists will understand that this system worked beautifully—until I bought so much thread that the shelves overflowed!

✓ **RAYON THREAD** is made by pressing cellulose acetate through small holes and then solidifying it in the form of filaments. It has a high sheen and is both soft and heat resistant. Unfortunately, it's not colorfast and neither as strong nor as durable as polyester.

✓ **METALLIC THREADS** are made of a core bonded with layers of rice paper for stability, silver alloy for shine, and an outside coating for easy handling. They come in a delightful variety of colors. When you are using metallic thread, keep in mind that you will have better results if you loosen the machine's upper tension one or more numbers, use a smooth, lint-free bobbin thread, and remember that this thread prefers a vertical spool pin. You may find that the most efficient way to determine the best tension is to reduce the top tension all the way to 0 and then slowly turn it up until you achieve smooth sewing. A simple and easy way to reduce the tension, especially useful when using more delicate threads, is to skip past the thread guide nearest the needle.

✓ Bonding layers of polyester together and slicing them to the desired size produces **FLAT-FILM POLYESTER THREAD**. This is definitely the showiest of all threads. It's also colorfast and heat resistant, but pretty much demands a vertical spool pin with a felt pad underneath so that it will rotate easily without kinking. Significantly lowering the tension, usually to a setting of 2 or 3, is also a good idea.

✓ **MONOFILAMENT THREADS** are not all the same. Polyester has a high heat tolerance and doesn't discolor or become brittle, while nylon tends to do both over time. Monofilament comes as either clear or smoke colored. When using it, reduce the top tension one or more numbers. It has to come off of the *top* of the spool, so it requires either a horizontal spool pin or must be placed in a cone thread holder behind your machine. When loading monofilament thread onto a bobbin, wind slowly in order to prevent stretching and be sure to wind the bobbin no more than about half full.

Heavy-Weight Threads (Tex 40–90)

Thread Type	Tex Size	In the Needle	In the Bobbin	Needle Type
Cotton or polyester	Tex 50 to 90	Heavy-weight cottons and polyesters	Same as the top thread; cotton thread 50/3 (Tex 35)	Topstitching 100/16 or 120/18
Silk	Tex 60	Silk #30	Silk #30; cotton 50/3 (Tex 35)	Sharp 90/14 or 100/16; denim or quilting 90/14
Cotton	Tex 50 Tex 60	30 weight thread 12 weight thread	30 weight thread 12 weight thread Cotton thread 50/3 (Tex 35)	Sharp, 90/14 or 100/16; demin or quilting 90/14
Cotton or polyester	Tex 40	Machine quilting 40/3	Same as top thread; machine embroidery thread 60/2 (Tex 18); cotton thread 50/3 (Tex 35)	Sharp, denim, or quilting 90/14
Rayon	Tex 40	Rayon #30	Rayon #30; machine embroidery thread 60/2 (Tex 18); cotton thread 50/3 (Tex 35)	Sharp, denim, embroidery, or quilting 90/14

Medium-Weight Threads (Tex 27–35)

Thread Type	TexSize	In the Needle	In the Bobbin	Needle Type
Cotton 50/60 Cotton 40/2	Tex 35	Cotton 50/3 or Tex 35	Same as the top thread; machine embroidery thread 60/2 (Tex 18)	Sharp or denim 80/12; quilting 75/11
Polyester 50/3	Tex 35	All purpose polyester	Same as top thread; machine embroidery thread 60/2 (Tex 18)	Sharp or denim 80/12; quilting 75/11
Silk Rayon	Tex 27	Silk #50 Rayon #35	Same as top thread; machine embroidery thread 60/2 (Tex 18)	Sharp or denim 80/12; embroidery 90/14

Light-Weight Threads (Tex 10–24)

Thread Type	TexSize	In the Needle	In the Bobbin	Needle Type
Metallic	Tex 24	Embroidery, 40 weight	Polyester or nylon bobbin thread	Metallic 70/11, 80/12, or 90/14
Rayon	Tex 24	Rayon #40	Same as top thread; machine embroidery thread 60/2 (Tex 18)	Sharp 60/10, 70/11, or 80/12; Denim 70/11 or 80/12; quilting 75/11
Acrylic or polyester	Tex 24	Embroidery	Same as top thread; machine embroidery thread 60/2 (Tex 18)	Sharp 70/11 or 80/12; quilting or embroidery 90/14
Cotton	Tex 18	Machine embroidery 60/2	Same as top thread	Sharp 60/10, 70/11, or 80/12; denim 70/11 or 80/12; quilting 75/11
Flat-film polyester	Tex 16	Flat film polyester	Nylon or polyester bobbin thread	Metallic 90/14
Cotton	Tex 10–12	Heirloom style threads	Same as top thread	Sharp 60/10 or 70/11 denim 70/11; quilting 75/11
Silk	Tex 12	Silk #100	Same as top thread	Sharp 60/10 or 70/11; denim 70/11; quilting 75/11
Polyester nylon	Tex 10	Monofiliament	Machine embroidery thread 60/2 (Tex 18); same as top thread	Sharp 60/10 or 70/11; denim 70/11; quilting 75/11

When selecting the correct needle for any project, consider these factors:

- Needle size—use small needles for lightweight fabrics and larger needles for heavier fabrics.
- Machine needles are numbered—the larger the number, the larger the needle (This is the exact opposite of hand-sewing needles.) Machine needles are usually marked with two numbers, for example 70/10. The larger number is the European size and the smaller is the American size. The number is printed on most needles in tiny print. (See the chart at the end of this section).
- Needle point—a sharp point is essential to ensure even stitch formation and avoid damaging the fabric.
- Needle suitability—be sure to use the needle that best fits *both* the fabric and the thread.

I usually place gently used needles back in the box on the left-hand side. This way I know everything about the needle and can successfully use it again.

Thread, Needle, and Bobbin Thread Combinations

The following tables offer some guidelines for making thread, needle, and bobbin thread choices. Remember that these are just suggestions. You may need to experiment in order to find what works for you and your machine. Also, consider that what works well today may not be the best choice tomorrow, so stay flexible. If you are a novice, start with the largest size needles and work your way down. If you are more experienced, start in the middle. My motto is that the *right* choice is the one that works right now!

Types of Machine Needles

Some brands of needles are color coded for easy identification, as follows:

✓ **QUILTING NEEDLE** (green)—a special taper to the point prevents damage to the sensitive, expensive materials used in quilting and makes it easier to sew seams.

✓ **JEANS/DENIM NEEDLE** (blue)—a needle with a sharp point meant for jeans and other densely woven materials. The coating and sharpness make a nice clean stitch.

✓ **MICROTEX/SHARP NEEDLE** (purple)—an extra sharp point for perfectly straight stitches, for use in topstitching or edge stitching applications.

✓ **MACHINE EMBROIDERY NEEDLE** (red)—designed with a special *scarf* and large eye to prevent shredding and breakage when sewing with rayon and specialty machine embroidery thread. Two threads can be used simultaneously in the 80 and 90 sizes. (The scarf is the indented area above the eye on the back of the needle, and it allows the bobbin hook to pass close to the needle to form the stitch.)

✓ **METALLICA NEEDLE** (no color on needle)—provides for trouble-free sewing with metallic threads. It has a large eye to make threading easier and a large groove to prevent shredding the delicate metallic threads during stitch formation.

✓ **TOPSTITCH NEEDLE** (no color on needle)—very sharp, with an extra large eye and a large groove to accommodate topstitch thread or more than one thread at a time. Use a topstitch needle where a larger eye size is beneficial, such as sewing with two threads through one needle. This needle, with its exceptionally large eye, is a good option when none other works.

Machine needles, left to right: Quilting 75/11 (green); Jeans/Denim 90/14 (blue); Microtex 70/10 (purple); Embroidery 90/14 (red); Metallica 80/12, Top Stitch 100/16, Double Embroidery 2.0/75.

When choosing heavy-weight threads, remember that they can make any project stiff and very "thready." Look at your project and consider the specific results that you want to achieve. If you are making a quilt or garment that needs to withstand heavy use, try putting the same heavy thread through the needle and in the bobbin. If you are using a heavy thread as an important part of your design, you will find the going much easier if the bobbin thread is somewhat lighter in weight.

The medium-weight threads listed in the next table are the easiest to use. They make great choices for the novice or anyone who is learning a new technique.

Light-weight threads are great for fancy stitching. They are very thin, so you can add a lot of thread to your project and "thready" doesn't become an issue.

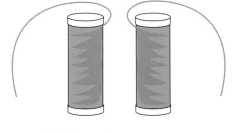

Double spools

Double Needles

Double needles sit two on a crossbar and are designed to be inserted into the machine at one time and sew the corresponding number of rows simultaneously. (Note, too, that three needles to a shaft are also available.)

Double needles are usually sized both according to the millimeters between the needles and by the size of the needles. They can be used with zigzag sewing machines that thread front to back. Keep in mind that when you use a double needle the stitching on the back is a zigzag because you have only one bobbin catching both top threads.

- Double denim needle—size: 4.0/100
- Double machine embroidery needle—sizes: 2.0/75 and 3.0/75
- Double metallica needle—sizes: 2.5/80 and 3.0/90

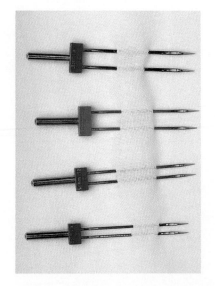

DOUBLE NEEDLES AND THEIR USES

Type	Size	Size in millimeters (distance between needles)	Use	Comment
Jeans/denim	100	4.0	Closely woven materials	For double stitching bias as in the stained-glass technique, or for decorative work on denim
Embroidery	75	2.0 3.0	Metallic and specialty threads	Special "scarf" and large eye to accommodate specialty threads when doing decorative work and pin-tucks
Metallica	80 90	2.5 3.0	Metallic threads	Designed for decorative double needle work

- Extra-wide double needle—for use in machines with at least a 6.0 mm stitch width. Sizes: 6.0/100 and 8.0/100

When using two spools of thread through the needle at the same time, be sure that the spools are placed as shown on the opposite page in order to prevent your threads from tangling.

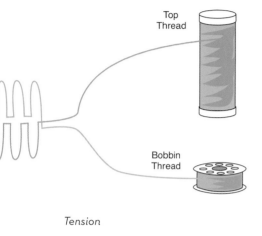

Tension

Tension

People are often afraid of the tension knob, but it's actually your best friend when you are machine sewing. Be bold about experimenting with different settings. I recommend making an informal sample for every combination of fabric and thread you plan to use. This need not be fancy—scraps of fabric and/or batting work just fine for this purpose. Thread the machine with your chosen top and bobbin threads. Select the appropriate needle, stabilizer, or decorative stitch, as necessary. Start with the normal tension setting and stitch a few inches. How does the stitching on the top look? How does it look on the bottom? Adjust the tension as needed. If you have loops on the bottom, adjust the top tension. If you have loops on the top, adjust the bottom tension.

***Clematis**, detail. Delicate machine embroidery threads are machine stitched for the quilting. See full quilt on page 99.*

Starts and Stops

In workshops and classes, one of the most frequent questions, asked by people at many levels of experience, concerns how best to start and stop machine sewing without resulting in unsightly stitches. The simplest solution is to make the usual set of 12 or so small stitches squeezed into a scant quarter inch, as any machine manual instructs, but to hide them in the ditch or well of the seam. Another option, when stitching a decorative design in a loop, for instance, is to make sure to stop and start in the exact same place. Sew the design with a regular stitch-length, then, when you return to your starting point, run these longer stitches right over the top of the short ones. Finish with another dozen tiny stitches over the regular stitches. The tiny stitches will not be visible.

If you really must avoid those unsightly stitch-starts and stops, you can always knot

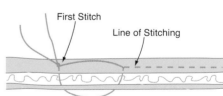

Start and stop knots

Prevent your fabric from slipping by wrapping the inner hoop.

your threads instead. Be sure to leave thread tails of about 3″ to 5″ long at either end of your line of stitches. Pull all the ends to the back and knot them. Sliding the threads into a large, easily threaded needle makes the task of burying the thread between the layers much quicker.

Stabilizing Your Fabric

A suitable stabilizer is necessary to prevent puckering when embellishing by machine. The stabilizer should be a lighter weight than the fabric. There are two ways to stabilize. You can use a hoop to hold the fabric in place temporarily and leave no lasting effect on it, or you can use a stabilizer that either adds stiffness or needs to be removed when the stitching is finished.

Quick and Easy Stabilizer

Spray starch makes an excellent, easy to use stabilizer. Liquid starch, mixed half-and-half with water in a spray bottle, is preferable to canned spray starch because the absence of foam means it doesn't flake. An easy way to remove any built up starch from the iron is to set a cold iron on a wet cloth for a few minutes. The starch wipes right off.

Stabilizing with a Hoop

Embroidery hoops come in many sizes. Six-, eight-, and ten-inch hoops are the easiest to use when machine sewing. They are large enough to allow plenty of stitching and small enough to fit within the confines of the sewing machine. Machine embroidery hoops are generally made of wood and are quite sturdy. They are narrower than hand hoops, which allows them to easily slip in and out under the needle. Wrapping the inner hoop with twill tape and

Machine stitchers need to remember to place the fabric on the bottom. If you are hand sewing, the opposite is true.

Troubleshooting

The more you machine sew, the easier you will find it to be, so have patience. There are a few general troubleshooting techniques that seem to solve most problems:
- Change the needle
- Use the right needle for the thread and the job (see page 104)
- Rethread the sewing machine, both needle and bobbin
- Clean your machine
- Sew more slowly

If the top thread breaks or shreds:
- The needle may be too small. It needs to be large enough to make a sufficient hole in the fabric to prevent wear on the thread.
- The needle tension may be too tight. Loosen the tension a little at a time until the thread stops breaking.
- Check to make sure the needle is properly installed.
- Some decorative threads become worn as they go through the thread guide on the machine closest to the needle. Skip this thread guide.
- Clean and oil your machine (check the manual).

Nylon mesh sleeves are a simple fix for slippery threads.

If you are using specialty threads, there are a few more issues to consider.
- If your metallic thread breaks, check to make sure you are using the correct needle. The bobbin thread type is also important. When you run your fingers down metallic thread, it feels a bit like fish scales. If you have a cotton thread in the bobbin, the metallic thread will constantly grab it and break. Switch to a polyester or nylon bobbin thread.
- Rayon and metallic threads tend to be slippery and fall off the spool. They may wind around the spool pin holder or catch on the spool itself. There are two possible solutions—a horizontal holder or a mesh or nylon sleeve for the thread.
- Adding a monofilament thread into the needle with very delicate metallic threads may add enough strength to the decorative thread to make sewing much easier.

If all else fails
- Ask your sewing machine dealer to check for burrs.

securing the end with glue increases the tension and helps hold the fabric without slipping.

For machine work, the fabric in the hoop must be taut across the bottom of the hoop. Tighten the screw until the material is like a drum, at the same time making sure it's straight and square.

Hoops used in conjunction with stabilizers are the best way to prevent distortion. Hoop the fabric and lay a stabilizer under it, holding it in place with a temporary spray adhesive or pins.

Stabilizers

Stabilizers are the secret ingredient that makes our work look professional. They can be placed either under or over the fabric and can be attached with or without a hoop. Each stabilizer has different characteristics. Stabilizers come in light-, medium-, and heavy-weight. If you feel you need a heavy-weight stabilizer, consider using two layers of light-weight stabilizer instead. This way you can tear the layers away one at a time and reduce the risk of damaging stitches. There are no hard and fast rules when working with them, but the following guidelines might help. Whichever stabilizer you choose, remember that for a professional, finished look, it's important that you iron your work frequently.

ABOVE, **Humble Administrator's Garden**, Melody Crust, 25″ × 54″. Stabilizers were absolutely essential in order to keep this design flat and square. LEFT, **Humble Administrator's Garden**, detail. Flowers done with a free motion zigzag stitch can have as much impact as you choose to give them.

- Use a tear-away (non-woven) stabilizer when there is no need for added stiffness in the finished product. An iron-on, tear-away stabilizer is useful when a hoop can't be used.
- Water-soluble stabilizer comes in sheets that wash out after the project is finished. No added stiffness or added filler will remain. Hot water stabilizers are used when no added stiffness can be tolerated in very dense embroidery. (Often this type of stitching is made entirely of thread after the stabilizer is melted away.)

- Liquid stabilizer, which can be painted or sprayed on, is used when a fabric can tolerate a liquid applied to it and when no hoop can be used. It washes out afterwards, so again, no added stiffness or filler remains.
- Permanent stabilizer should be used when the stitching needs added support after completion. The stabilizer may be an organdy or other non-woven type of fabric and remains permanently part of the project.
- Iron-on fusible web is used to attach one fabric to another.
- Tissue, craft, or quilt marking papers are all inexpensive, removable stabilizers.

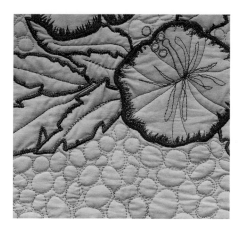

Humble Administrator's Garden, detail. Layering two light-weight cut-away stabilizers allowed me to tear each one off separately without damaging my stitching. See full quilt on page 109.

Simple machine embroidery with heavy purple or green needle thread, using a quilting design for the pattern, is supported by a light-weight cut-away stabilizer.

MACHINE STITCHING TECHNIQUES

Now that you have the basic knowledge of the materials and equipment used for decorative sewing by machine, let's explore the diversity of specific techniques that apply to either the top layer or through the layers of a project.

Machine Appliqué

Applique done by machine can replicate the look of hand appliqué or add the extra pizzazz of decorative stitching. Metallic or contrasting thread lends highlights to the appliqué while matching or invisible thread is very subtle.

Raw-edge appliqué is perhaps the simplest form—just fuse and press. Of course, in order to secure the edges, some form of stitching is necessary. A free motion straight or zigzag stitch will work beautifully. The fusing supplies extra stiffness so no extra stabilizer is needed.

Other possibilities are satin and zigzag stitching. To satin stitch, adjust the stitch regulator to the shortest possible length and select the width adjustment you prefer. You might want to start with the automatic width and go from there to see what you like. Inside and outside corners can be tricky, so be sure to practice. A stabilizer is probably going to be necessary, so add one to your practice sample.

The blanket stitch is another stitch successfully done by machine. Make a practice sample. Try using the traditional black thread or maybe this is the time to pull out that new variegated thread you just bought.

The blind hem stitch best replicates hand appliqué and is a stitch available on many zigzag machines. Adjust the blind hem stitch length and width to about .5. Monofiliment thread is used through the needle. Matching cotton machine embroidery thread in the bobbin is a good choice, but monofiliament is also an option. This small stitch swings to the side and "bites" the patch to be appliqued. The needle then makes three or four stitches in the background, followed by another swing stitch. It takes a little practice, but the results are well worth the effort.

The easiest way to get a heavy thread look is to use two threads in the needle at the same time.

Machine Embroidery

Long, more or less straight, lines can be stitched without a hoop. Just a touch of starch stiffens the fabric enough for simple stitching. Other decorative stitches on your machine might give your work a new and fresh look. By all means, experiment!

Free-motion embroidery appliqués are done in a hoop with synthetic organza and a heavy-weight water-soluble stabilizer. Draw as many designs on the stabilizer as will fit in the hoop. Set your machine for free-motion straight stitch, then stitch a very small zigzag around the shape. Stitch back and forth in both directions, making a grid that includes the outline stitching. Over these base stitches, fill in until the desired denseness of thread is reached. Stitch all of your designs. After dissolving the stabilizer you will have wonderful, personal appliqués.

Red work, traditionally done by hand, can be also stitched by machine. Hoop your fabric, insert red thread (perhaps a 12-weight cotton) through the needle and red thread in the bobbin, then stitch. It's easy, fun, and quick to sew.

Redesign Your Fabric—with Thread

Adding thread to fabric is a technique that machine stitchers sometimes overlook. A simple line of thread can add interest or a bit of sparkle. Consider sewing a double row of stitches onto a quilt top, or perhaps do some free motion embroidery on preprinted fabric.

A couple of things to keep in mind are that a good-looking straight stitch is flat and pucker free and that stitching is easier if the same color thread is in both the

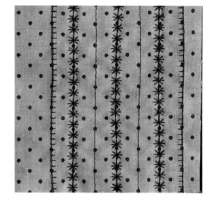

Using the dots to keep the decorative stitches even, red machine embroidery thread, a #75 quilting needle, and a light-weight tear-away stabilizer combine to make a personalized fabric.

needle and the bobbin. That way any bobbin thread poking up from the bottom won't show.

Thread embellishment is easy to do with a zigzag stitch, either with or without a presser foot. A zigzag stitch can turn into a plaid when stitched in both directions. This same stitch pattern changes dramatically when more than one color of thread is used.

Many sewing machines today have a variety of designs preprogrammed into the machine. Here are a few techniques to consider:

• Try increasing the length of your stitch.
• Sewing on the vertical grain produces a tidier, more professional looking piece.
• Press frequently for a smooth, finished look.
• Use the needle-down position, if available. By maintaining your "place" in your work, you avoid distorting the design.

Free-motion stitching is accomplished by lowering or covering the feed dogs and using a darning foot. You are feeding the fabric without the aid of the

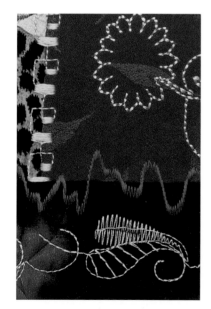

Programmed stitches made the leaves and flowers. The orange stitching was done free motion after setting my machine to zigzag.

Chatty Blossoms, detail. To embellish successfully, I need to have a plan in mind. Here the green sash is the trellis and the couching threads represent the vines winding around it. See full quilt on page 96.

machine, making this an exercise in hand, foot, and eye coordination. It takes a bit of practice. You have complete control over the length of your stitches. If the stitches are too short, either slow the speed of the machine or move your fabric faster. Long stitches require just the opposite; either push the fabric slower or increase the speed of the machine.

It may increase your precision if you engage the needle-down feature, if your machine has it. I suggest that you use the half- or slower-speed option, if your machine has one.

Any technique that can be accomplished when quilting can be done over the surface, but since you are working without the stiffness supplied by the batting and backing material, you will need a way to stabilize your fabric (see page 109).

Machine Sashiko

This traditionally hand-sewn technique is easy to replicate with your machine. A large-eye needle, heavy white thread, a long stitch (4 to 8 per inch), and a bobbin thread to match the fabric will do the trick. The object is for the bobbin thread to break the surface of the white thread, in order to look like hand stitching and you may need to play with the tension control in order to achieve this. While white is the traditional look, don't feel bound to it. Different colored threads dramatically affect the look of this stitching.

Traditional sashiko is usually a very linear design stitched by hand on indigo fabric. This machine design was drawn using a ruler and pencil. Place a stabilizer under the denim, set the stitch length long, thread your needle with a heavier white cotton thread, put a medium-weight thread in the bobbin, and sew. Taking the time to plan your path of stitching makes this an easy project.

Machine Couching

A very dynamic way to add dimension, texture, and color to your fabric is machine couching. *Couching* is simply a method of stitching over cord, yarn, braid, ribbon, or decorative thread without puncturing it.

Specialty presser feet make couching painless. Cording feet have holes that allow the couched cord to pass through as you stitch. These feet may have one or many holes, which keep the cord and stitching in line, resulting in the illusion of ribbon.

The needle thread can be identical to the couched ribbon, cord, or other embellishment, or it can provide a contrast. Invisible thread puts the emphasis on the ribbon or cord, while a contrasting color or a shiny metallic thread will become a noticeable element in the overall design. Whatever thread you choose, be careful to secure and hide the ends. Either plan to hide them in the seam, cover them with other stitching, or pull them to the back and tie a knot to secure them.

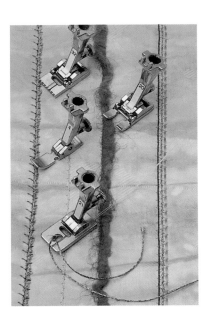

Use a dental floss threader to pull the couching material through the hole of the cording foot.

The only downside to couching by machine is the back of the work will be messy. Fortunately, couching worked on the top layer of the fabric gives you the opportunity to hide the mess between the layers.

Crazy Quilting by Machine

Crazy quilts are as unique as their creators. A technique usually done by hand, it's easy to duplicate with your machine. This is definitely the time to show off your thread collection! Built-in decorative stitches automatically lend themselves to hundreds of design possibilities by combining your favorite stitches and threads.

Use any fabric combination of texture and color to create your own one-of-a-kind heirloom. Making these quilts is a great way to have fun with old silk ties, fancy fabric dress scraps, velvets, and all kinds of ribbons and laces. Sewing machines can make this a quick and easy process. If you make crazy quilts, or just crazily quilted objects, using metallic and other decorative threads may be easier when sewn by machine.

Bernina Bag, Melody Crust. An incredible new embroidery sewing machine was the inspiration for this purse. The amazing variety of stitches it offered and my thread collection let me run wild.

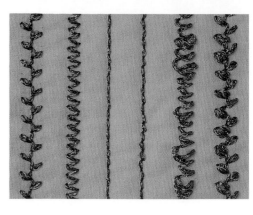

Stitching from the Bobbin

Did you know that thread that is too thick to fit through a needle can be machine stitched from the bobbin? The stitching is actually done from the back. While it can sometimes be frustrating to use thread with a thick and/or bumpy surface that can only be wound on the bobbin a little at a time, the results can certainly make it all worthwhile.

What a difference! The threads on the left were placed through the bobbin tension guide. The loosely stitched threads on the right skipped the bobbin tension altogether.

Wind thick thread onto a bobbin, either by hand or machine. Choosing to skip the bobbin tension is one of the simplest, no-fail places to play with thread tension. If you put the heavy bobbin thread through the tension guide, you will get a totally different look. The bobbin tension screw must be loosened. Place the bobbin over a white paper towel before you adjust it to ensure against losing the tiny screw. Think of the screw as a clock face and turn it one hour to start. Just a very little can make a big difference. Turn to the left to loosen and to the right to tighten (remember: *lefty loosy, righty tighty*). Consult your machine manual for other systems. It's a good idea to buy a second bobbin case for this use because the thicker thread can stretch the tension spring.

Most threads stitched from the bobbin are successful when done with a straight stitch. Some just won't cooperate unless you sew free motion or with programmed stitching. Experiment to see what works best for you.

Tropical Garden, *detail. Stitching from the back offers the opportunity to quilt with heavy threads that don't fit through the needle. This red flower is a very heavy rayon thread stitched from the back. See full quilt on page 124.*

Threads that lend themselves to stitching from the back vary greatly, but the ones with a somewhat smoother finish work best. Some heavy threads will only cooperate with a straight stitch or on gentle curves. Others are happy with free motion. Be sure to make a sample to see what works for you.

THREADS FOR BOBBIN STITCHING

Bobbin Thread	Top Thread	Comment
Perle Crown Rayon	Rayon	Lustrous, good for free motion
Perle Crown Cotton	50 weight cotton	Matte finish, good for free motion
Metallic Threads	Smooth metallic	Sparkly, generally good for free motion
Braids	Nylon or polyester bobbin thread	Rich, good for large programmed stitches
Plied Threads	Rayon	Beautiful sheen, good for straight stitching

LEFT, *Pre-stamped cross-stitch kit, Rex W. Waldron, 82″ × 96″. Sometimes a pre-stamped pattern exactly fits your mood and produces beautiful results like this. It can also be a perfect "away from home" project because you can pretty well predict what materials you will need.* ABOVE, *Cross-stitch, detail. A simple design, but oh, so lovely!*

Caring for Machine-Stitched Projects

Believe it or not, different threads have different needs when it comes to cleaning your work. In general, it's safe to machine wash or dry clean threads, although there are a few notable exceptions. Rayon thread has a high sheen and is heat resistant so you can machine wash it, but it isn't colorfast and can fade over time. Never use rayon threads in applications that might be bleached. Nylon monofilament may melt under an iron and in some high temperature dryers.

HAND STITCHING

Many of us hand sew simply because we like it. There is often great comfort and satisfaction in the quiet rhythm of sliding a needle in and out of fabric. And, obviously, most hand sewing projects are considerably more portable than their machine sewn cousins. In addition, there are many surface techniques that, by their very nature, require that they be implemented by human hand. The biggest difference between machine and hand applied thread is the thickness of the line. A machine stitched line is a solid strand of thread, while the dashes of a hand stitched line are much more subtle.

Blue Bag, Melody Crust. A Crazy bag hand embellished with crazy quilting can be made richer with decorative stitching, buttons, and trims.

Prep Work and Supplies

There is no need for many special supplies beyond the tools already in your sewing kit. Nor is there much to be done in the way of preparation. All this makes hand sewing an easy and relaxing option, especially for take-along projects.

Selecting Hand-Sewing Threads

Most of the threads discussed in the machine sewing section (see page 104) can be successfully sewn by hand. One exception might be metallic thread, which can a bit of a challenge. The stress the eye of a hand-sewing needle puts on this delicate thread can cause it to break repeatedly. You are likely to have much better luck sewing metallic thread by machine, making sure to use the correct needle.

Whatever thread or floss you choose, resist the urge to put a long length of it on your needle. Using a short, 18″ to 24″ length really helps prevent tangling. For best results when hand sewing, consider the following thread types.

- *Perle cotton* is a highly mercerized, twisted, non-divisible and lustrous cotton thread. It's available in sizes 3, 5, 8 and 12, comes in many colors, and is 100 percent cotton. (Mercerized means that the thread has been specially treated to make it stronger, glossier, and more color-saturated.)
- *Metallic perle cotton*, a twisted, metallic thread, is available in size 5 only. It comes in either gold or silver and is non-divisible.

All of these gorgeous threads, designed for hand sewing, and many, many more, can definitely spice up any project.

- *Wool floss* is a versatile thread that can be worked using a single strand for delicate stitching or several strands can be combined to create a more dramatic effect. It is 100 percent wool, available in a huge range of colors and is both colorfast and mothproof.
- *Rayon floss* is a lustrous, six-strand, divisible thread that is particularly striking.
- *Metallic embroidery floss*, a six-strand metallic thread, is a beautiful, shiny thread ideal for all types of stitchery. It is divisible, so you can use one strand to blend or several strands for a stunning effect.
- *Six-strand cotton embroidery floss* is the most common thread used for embroidery. It's inexpensive and is available just about everywhere. This floss comes in a huge array of colors, both solid and variegated.
- *Silk floss* adds a special elegance to any project and is available in many colors.

Chinese embroidery and thread. Chinese women buy this preprinted fabric and then embroider it to make unique clothing.

Storing Hand-Sewing Threads

Store threads away from light and dust like all other materials in your studio. Put them in cardboard boxes that allow the threads to breathe rather than in plastic ones. Use drawers rather than open shelves. Many of my hand sewing threads are stored in old silverware trays tucked into drawers, which is a tidy way to keep the colors easy to find and always at hand.

Selecting Hand-Sewing Needles

There is a bewildering array of needles from which to choose. Type and size classify hand-sewing needles, with each designed for a specific use. One size definitely does not fit all! Be sure to choose the type of needle according to the job it will perform and the size according to the thread it will hold. Keep in mind that for hand-sewing needles, the higher the number, the smaller the needle (the opposite of machine needles).

- *Betweens* or *Quilting*: very short, round-eyed needles, used to make fine, short, sturdy stitches. Because these needles are thick, they can better withstand the stress of stitching through the multiple layers of a quilt. I suggest starting with an 8 or 9 and gradually progressing to an 11 or 12 as you become more proficient and your stitches become more even.
- *Sharps*: all-purpose, medium length needles with small round eyes commonly used for appliqué and general sewing. These are an excellent choice for fine embroidery and hand sewing because they are easy to thread and slide through fabric with a minimum of effort.
- *Straw* or *Milliner*: long and slender with small rounded eyes. Many quilters like them for appliqué because their flexibility aids in maneuvering the fabric. Their thinness also makes them a good option for embroidering French knots.

Hand-sewing needles, left to right: Between size 10, Sharp size 11, Straw size 10, Chenille size 18, Tapestry size 18, Embroidery size 3, Beading size 10, and Easy Threading size 4.

Hand Sewing Threads and Needles

Type of Needle	Common Sizes	Use	Type of Thread
Betweens or quilting	5 to 12	Quilting Beading Straight stitch Appliqué	Quilting thread Nymo thread Embroidery floss Any heavier machine thread used for quilting
Sharps	10, 11, 12	General sewing Appliqué Couching	Regular sewing thread Any thread used for appliqué (silk, machine embroidery thread) Threads used for couching (metallic, rayon, invisible or any other thread used to hold a very heavy thread on the surface
Straw or milliners	3 to 11	Appliqué	Any thread used for applique (silk, machine embroidery thread)
Chenille	18 to 24	Silk ribbon work	Quilting thread Embroidery floss Any heavier thread (including silk ribbon) that needs a larger hole in order to prevent crushing the thread
Tapestry	13 to 26	Any stitching requiring a dull-pointed needle that won't pierce other threads or yarn	Decorative thread
Embroidery (Crewel)	1 to 0	Embroidery Embellishing Appliqué Red work	Embroidery floss Any heavier machine thread Any heavier hand-sewing thread
Beading	10 to 13	Beading	Nymo
Easy threading	4 to 8	Machine quilters use these for hiding thread tails in between the layers	Any

Threading and Knotting

Threading Tips

Barbara, a charming and active 80-something, is a favorite quilting friend. She confided to me that she was so frustrated by needle-threading difficulties, she was thinking of giving up quilting. I was happy to share these tips, which might make your sewing easier, too.

- Different spools of thread are wound differently, so when you cut off a piece, look to see on which end the fibers stay together. Thread this end first.
- Knot the end that you did not put through the needle. This way if the needle falls off the thread, you can rethread the easier end back through.
- Wet the needle not the thread.
- The eye of the needle is made by a stamping process that leaves a larger opening on one side than the other. Thread through the larger side.
- Thread a supply of needles in the morning while your eyes are fresh.
- Place something white behind the needle so you can see more clearly.
- Buy a good needle threader.
- When all else fails, have someone else thread a supply of needles for you!

Quilter's Knots

Once mastered, a quilter's knot is one guaranteed to be the same size. This is a real advantage when you want to "pop" the knot through your fabric to hide it.

1. Point the two ends toward each other. I think of jousting.
2. Wrap the thread around the needle. The same number of wraps every time will mean the knot is the same size every time.
3. Pull the needle through the wraps (this is just like making a French knot). You should have a perfect knot!

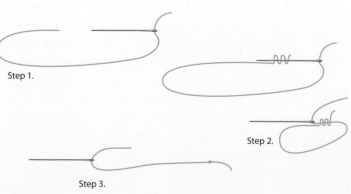

Step 1.

Step 2.

Step 3.

Quilter's knot

- *Chenille*: short, thick needles with long, oval eyes and sharp points. The longer eye allows multiple strands of embroidery floss, pearl cotton, or silk ribbon to be easily threaded. The over-sized needle makes a larger hole in the fabric and helps prevent you from unintentionally crushing silk ribbon or large thread by forcing it through a too-small hole.
- *Tapestry*: short and thick with a large eye and blunt point. The long oval eye carries silk ribbon and other bulky threads easily. These needles are often used for wrapped stitches (where the first line of stitching is laid down as usual and a second thread is wrapped around it, staying on the surface of the fabric) because the dull point doesn't pierce the original thread.
- *Embroidery (crewel)*: medium length with long, oval eyes. They have two advantages; the long eye ensures easy threading and the very sharp point pierces closely woven fabrics with less effort.
- *Beading*: extra long and fine with a small round eye. Generally they are used for beading due to their flexibility. This very long, very flexible needle is hard to control when stitching through fabric so it's usually used for stringing beads, not for applying them.
- *Easy threading*: relatively large needles used when threading needles is a problem. Machine quilters who tie knots will find these needles handy when burying thread a knot tail after it is tied.

Chatty Blossoms, detail. This variation of traditional appliqué employs the straight stitch. The thread is intended to show just because I liked the way it looked. See full quilt on page 96.

HAND-SEWING TECHNIQUES

It's simply amazing what can be accomplished with just a threaded needle! There are so many different stitches and techniques available for you to use. Let's explore some of the possibilities.

Hand Appliqué

Adding embroidered details to an appliqué is a great way to create interest. French knots look great as flower centers and a stem stitch works very nicely as leaf veins. For extra dimension and definition, try chain stitching a decorative border.

Straight stitch appliqué is a fast and easy technique—just turn under the edges of the appliqué and straight stitch it onto your project. The stitch might be a simple one, but the end result can be spectacular. Use metallic threads or glow-in-the-dark threads to create a spider's web. Try pearlized or icy-blue thread for snow effects, or glistening metallic ribbons to create dew-kissed flowers.

Another great option is the old-fashioned but still popular blanket stitch. Traditionally done with two or three strands of black embroidery floss, it can be livened up by using perle cotton instead. And, of course, you aren't limited to just black. Blanket stitching is easy—just bring the needle up at A, hold the thread with your left thumb, go down at B and come up at C.

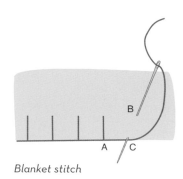

Blanket stitch

Bedtime Story, *Patricia Michelsen, quilted by Noell Pfaff, 48" × 61". Pat's beautiful hand embroidery exemplifies all the best qualities of red work.*

Hand Embroidery

Machines can emulate fine handwork, but none can exactly duplicate it. By its nature, embroidery places the emphasis on the thread. A good example is red work, which is stitching with red thread on a white background. A departure from this traditional style might be white thread stitched on a red background or using multi-colored thread. All are unique and beautiful alternatives. There are so many fun and effective decorative hand embroidery stitches that can have an amazing impact on your finished design.

Backstitch

Backstitching is easy—bring your needle up at A, down at B, up at C, and continue on. Backstitch with two or three strands of floss. Stitches should be the same length throughout, except on tight curves and small shapes, where you will need to shorten your stitches to make the lines smooth. Adding a thin cotton batting to the fabric before you sew contributes a third dimension and also helps conceal the knots.

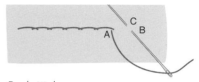

Backstitch

***Running Wild**, Melody Crust, 40" × 48". Sometimes a twist on traditional techniques makes for a fresh new look. This is red work in reverse; three strands of white embroidery floss are worked on red fabric.*

ABOVE, **English Tea**, Melody Crust, 30" × 15". Many quilters use embroidery floss, but don't let the thread limit your design possibilities. This thread is a thick, variegated polyester made especially for machine stitching. RIGHT, **English Tea**, detail.

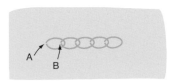

Chain stitch

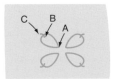

Lazy Daisy

Chain Stitch

Create a chain stitch by bringing the needle up and down at A, leaving a small loop of thread. Go up at B, passing the needle through the loop and then back down, again leaving a loop, to start the next stitch. I consider this one of the most versatile embroidery stitches. You can use it to do anything, ranging from adding another color just because you like it to obscuring seam lines.

Lazy Daisy Stitch

To make a Lazy Daisy stitch, push your needle up and down at A, leaving a small loop. Come up at B, pass the needle through the loop, then down at C. This is a fast and simple way to add impact by making great flowers or accents for beads or buttons.

French Knot

Start by bringing the needle up where you want to place your knot. Hold the thread with your weaker hand. Wrap the thread three times (more for a larger knot) around the needle. Holding some tension on the thread, insert the

needle next to the "up" spot, then pull it through the fabric to form the knot. You control the size and texture of the knot. Thick thread and lots of wraps around the needle provide a much bigger impact than thin thread and fewer wraps.

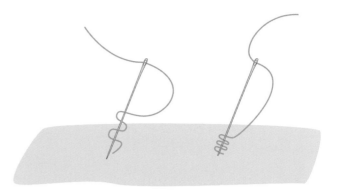

French Knot

Hand Sashiko

Sashiko originated with Japanese women who needed to make warm garments long before the days of central heating. It was simply a means of stitching two pieces of heavy fabric together using fine running stitches in order to reinforce them and repair damaged fabrics, but evolved into a very decorative art form.

Traditional patterns tend to be linear. Mark the design with a ruler and a chalk marker, then layer and stitch using the running stitch. Sashiko is very dramatic with highly contrasting thread and fabric colors, as in the traditional dark indigo blue and white. For a more subtle look just employ less contrast.

Hand Couching

Couching done by hand is accomplished by arranging braid, ribbon, yarn, or heavy threads that are too large to easily pass through the fabric in a design on the top of it. Then make small spiral stitches around, then under, the arranged braid or other embellishment, thus attaching it to the fabric. Experiment! Try using threads of contrasting colors, weights, and textures to achieve different results.

Crazy Quilting by Hand

Webster's Dictionary defines a crazy quilt as a patchwork quilt with no regular design. However, the term *crazy quilting* is something of a misnomer. It doesn't so much refer to the actual combining of layers that construct a quilt, but rather describes a unique conglomeration of randomly pieced fabrics with embroidered embellishments on nearly every seam and patch. Crazy quilting has its roots in an era when needlework was one of the few acceptable pastimes for women. It became a status symbol because only women who could afford hired help had the time to devote to fancy stitchery.

You can really jazz up your project by putting decorative stitches over the seams, couching over one or more cords or ribbons and adding beads or buttons for texture. Other ideas are to duplicate rows of stitching, highlight them with an entirely different stitch or use thread to work a specific design onto your fabric. Crazy quilting is the ultimate in handwork, but it's like eating chocolate. Once you start, it's hard to stop!

Tropical Garden, *Melody Crust, 40″ × 58″. Choosing the appropriate needle and thread ensures good results every time.*

Caring for Hand-Stitched Projects

Most threads used for hand stitching can be machine washed or dry-cleaned. The one notable exception is silk floss, which needs to be dry cleaned.

IDEA GALLERY

By now your **MIND** is spinning with new **IDEAS** on how you can get even more **CREATIVE** with **THREAD** than you already are! The following are examples of styles and **TECHNIQUES** that I really **ENJOY.** Hopefully, you'll see something new that entices you to **TRY** it.

Tropical Garden, Melody Crust, 40″ × 58″. Choosing the appropriate needle and thread ensures good results every time.

Tropical Garden, detail. The flower shapes were quilted through the layers and the brown centers were hand embroidered after the fact. See full quilt on page 124.

Machine couching with invisible thread and a blind hem stitch lets the beauty of the cord shine through.

Hand embroidery attaches the ribbons, giving them a nice, finished look.

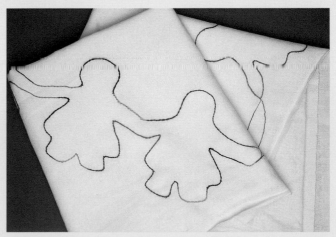

Tea towels are wonderfully easy to embellish by hand or machine. Instead of floss, I used a heavy polyester variegated thread that makes it look like a lot more work than it actually was. The dolls were hand stitched and the gentle curves stitched by machine.

IDEA GALLERY

The stitching added to this pre-printed fish appliqué personalizes the quilt and, at the same time, adds an interesting fish-scale detail.

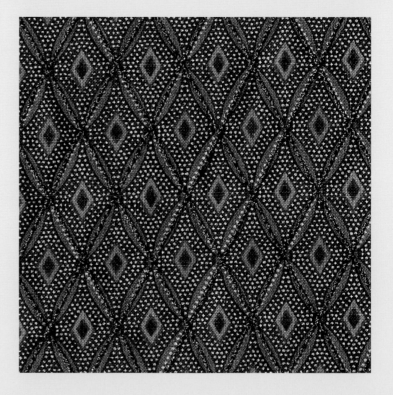

This stitched-over-the-surface fabric was facilitated with lightweight iron-on interfacing. Heavy purple metallic thread was couched with a small zigzag stitch using matching embroidery thread through both the needle and the bobbin.

Variegated rayon thread and a feather stitch for quilting are all the adornment necessary.

This is a very forgiving programmed stitch common to most machines. It's easier and more interesting than stitching in the ditch, especially when used with a variegated thread.

IDEA GALLERY

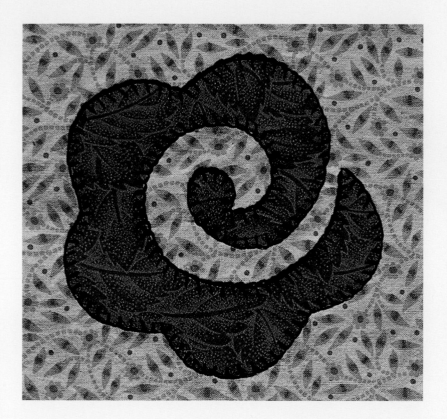

Flower appliqués are made easy by a light-weight fusible web. The three strands of black embroidery floss and a blanket stitch done by hand finish this traditional technique.

The curvy programmed stitch and free motion flower are bobbin quilted (from the back) with hand-dyed rayon in the bobbin and invisible thread through the needle.

Simple yet effective! Fusible web on the floral fabric, cut out and machine stitched to the background, is enhanced by black embroidery thread.

Bobbin stitching over the surface is much easier when your fabric is heavily starched. This sample has hand-dyed rayon in the bobbin paired with invisible thread in the needle.

My favorite flower blossom is stem stitched by hand using three strands of embroidery floss. The addition of a thin batting adds dimension and hides all of the knots.

Blanket stitched baskets are easy to sew when done before piecing or quilting. The basket handles are just free motion stitched to incorporate a bit of whimsy.

RESOURCES

I encourage you to support your local quilt shops, but if you cannot find products locally the sources listed below are available to all. These are my personal favorites, but a quick search on the web will yield several more options.

SEWING MACHINES AND SUPPLIES

Bernina of America, Inc.
www.berninausa.com
630-978-2500

PAINTS

Jacquard Products
www.jacquardproducts.com
800-442-0455

PRO Chemical & Dye
www.prochemical.com
800-2-BUY-DYE

INKS

Tsukineko Inc.
www.tsukineko.com
425-883-7733

Jean Hansen
(for Shiva brand paint sticks)
www.jeanhansen.com
800-399-4276

FOIL

Jones Tones
www.jonestones.com
800-216-0616

THREADS

Superior Threads
www.superiorthreads.com
800-499-1777

Kreinik Mfg. Co., Inc.
www.kreinik.com
800-537-2166

Web of Thread, Inc.
www.webofthread.com
800-955-8185

Speed Stitch, Inc.
www.speedstitch.com
866-829-7235

Uncommon Thread, Inc.
www.uncommonthread.com
877-294-5427

Elin Noble (hand-dyed threads)
www.ElinNoble.com
508-763-3593

INDEX

Appliqué   126, 128

Backstitch   43, 121
Basting   80
Beading   38
   beads
      care and storage of   41–42
      placement   42–43
      pre-testing   41
      shopping for   39
      varieties of   38–40
   buttons   47
   by hand   43–47
      basic stitch   44
      bugle fence   45
      bugle stacking   45
      couching   45–46
      fringes and dangles   46
      grouped   45
      locking   46
      loops   46
      picots   47, 48
      scalloped edge   47
      scattering   45
      straight and curved lines   45
   by machine   47
      couching   48
      free motion   49
   prep work for   38
   supplies   38–39
Bias tape 81, 82–83
   fusible   83
   prep work for   81
Blanket stitch   119, 128
Bobbin stitching   129
Brayer   12
Button holes, decorating   59
Buttons   56
   beading   47
   embellishing   57–59, 63
      covered   58
   prep work for   56
   selecting   57
   supplies   56–57

Care and cleaning   26
   for crystals   55
   for hand-stitched projects   123
   for machine-stitched projects   115
   for pearls   51
   for ribbons   71, 81

for silk   86
for thread   102
for trim-embellished projects   85
Chain stitch   122
Cord   83, 94
   making   83, 84
Couching 126
   by hand 45–46
   by machine   48, 112–113
      free motion   48
   of ribbon   76
Crayons   16
   prep work for   16
   rubbings   18

Embellishing garments   52–53

Fabrics, embellishing with   85–89
   doilies   86, 95
   handkerchiefs   86–87
   lace   87
   lamé 88
   polyesters   88–89
      heat cutting   89
   prep work for   85
   silk   88
      care of   86
   ultra-suede   89, 94
   velvet   87
      embossing of   87–88
Foiling   22
   adhesives for   23
   burnishing of   23
   heat application   24
   prep work for   22
   supplies   22
French knot   122, 123
Fringe   83   (see also Beading)
Fusible web   24, 109, 128   (see also
   Stabilizing fabric)

Hand (of fabric)   7
Heat-setting   (see also Hot-fix crystals)
   foils   24
   inks   21
   marking pens   20
   paints   9, 10, 16
Highlighting   10   (see also Outlining)
Hoop, embroidery   39, 110
   Stabilizing with 108–109
Hot-fix crystals   55

appliqués   55
tool for   56

Inks, using   20
   prep work for   21
   Tsukineko   21
   water color effects   21

Jewels   50, 53–54   (see also Hot-fix
   crystals)
   prep work for   50
   rhinestones   53

Labeling   20, 61, 95

Marking pens   18, 20   (see also Inks,
   using)
   freehand design   20
   lettering   19
   prep work for   19

Needles, hand   117–119
Needles, machine
   double needles, using   106–107
   selecting   103
   types 104–105

Outlining 18, 35

Paints   6
   acrylic   8
   checkerboard pattern, creating   11
   color blending   7
   for fabrics   7, 9, 11
      transparent   10, 35
      opaque   10
      metallic   10
   outlining with   35
   paint sticks 14, 15
   prep work for   6, 15
   salt, using 12
   spray   11
   supplies   8, 15
   white on white   35
   yardage   11
Pearls   50–51
   prep work for   50

Quilter's knot   118
Quilts illustrated
   Abstract   7

All Dressed for School 66
Baltimore Revisited 18
Bedtime Story 120
Benjamin Bunny 7
Beauties in a Basket 91
Buttons, Bangles and Bows 72
Camille 95
Cape Cod Cherries 34
Chatty Blossoms 96
China Cabinet 86
Clematis 99
Cosmic Dreams 24
Daisy Delight 33
Duchess 50
English Tea 122
Eye Candy - bugle edge 38
Eye Candy with Buttons 67
Eye Candy with Eyelash Trim 81
Eye Candy, Ribbon Binding 93
Eye Candy with Six Point Fringe 64
Eye Candy, Trim Edge 93
Eye Candy with Yellow Full Fringe 67
Eye Candy with Yellow Picot Edge 48
Fairyland 98
Fantasia 29
Fear No Color 101
Galaxy 22
Garden Party 89
Garden Windows, Bendigo 36
Heebee Jeebee 57
Halo 23
Hugs and Love 74
Humble Administrator's Garden 109
Imperial Flowers 15
It Dawned on Me 72
The Jewel 68
Lavish Leaf 31
Love Potion 62
Mardi Gras 42
Mirabella 60
Neptune's Weave 49
New Year's Eve 80
Nighttime 6
Painted Desert 9
Pears 13
Pink Perfection 67
Plum Blossoms 51
Pretty Maids All in Row 73
Reflections 54
Running Wild 121
Soles 12
Spotlight 43
Sunscape 30
Sunstream 95

Sweet Potato Vine 25
Tart Sweet 100
Tropical Garden 118
View from the Top 30
Wild About Flowers 56
Wild Flowers 47
Xishaungbanna 4

Red work 111, 121
Ribbon 70
    applications 76-81
        couching 76
        flowers and rosettes 76-78
        leaves and stems 78-79
        ruching 76, 93
    basting 80
    bows 79
    care of 71, 81
    embroidery of 79
    fabric made from 79
    prep work for 71-72
    sewing with 81
    supplies 70
    types 72-76
Rick rack 81, 82, 94, 95
    prep work for 81
Ruching 76, 90

Sashiko 112
    by hand 123
Sequins 50, 51-52
    attaching by hand 52
    attaching by machine 53
    prep work for 50
Shishas 50, 54
    attaching by hand 54
    attaching by machine 54
    prep work for 50
Stabilizing (of fabric) 108-109, 111
    embroidery hoop, using 108-109
    fabric painting 8
Stamping 12
Stenciling 25-27
    making stencils 27
    with marker pens 19
Stitching, hand 115
    basting 80
    beading 43-47
    caring for projects 123
    couching 45-46, 123
    crazy quilting 123
    prep work for 116
    sashiko 123
    sequins 52

supplies 116
techniques 119, 121-123
    appliqué 119
    embroidery 121-123, 125
Stitching, machine 98
    bobbin, using 114
    threads for 114
    caring for projects 115
    prep work for 98
    selecting thread 99
    starts and stops 107
    techniques 110-114
        appliqué 110
        couching 112-113, 125
        crazy quilting 113
        embellishment 111
        embroidery 110
            free-motion 111-112
            programmed 111, 127, 128
        red work 111
        sashiko 112
    supplies 99
    troubleshooting 108
Straight stitch appliqué 119
Sun printing 12
Supplies needed
    beading 38-39
    buttons 56-57
    fabric painting 8, 15
    foiling 22
    hand stitching 116
    machine stitching 99
    ribbon 70

Tassels 84
Thread
    changing 101
    cross-wound vs. straight wound 101
    measurement of 100
    selecting for hand stitching 116, 118
    selecting for machine stitching 99
    storing, hand 117
    storing, machine 102
    types of 102-104
Threading and knotting 118
Three-dimensional effects 90-91
    gathering 90, 91
    prairie points 90
    ruching 90
    yo-yos 91
Transferring 9
    crayons 17

Wrap knot 85